Detailed Mandala Coloring Book For Relaxation

Detailed Mandala Patterns Coloring Pages

Sandra Bacon

Detailed Mandala Coloring Book For Relaxation
Copyright © 2019 By Sandra Bacon

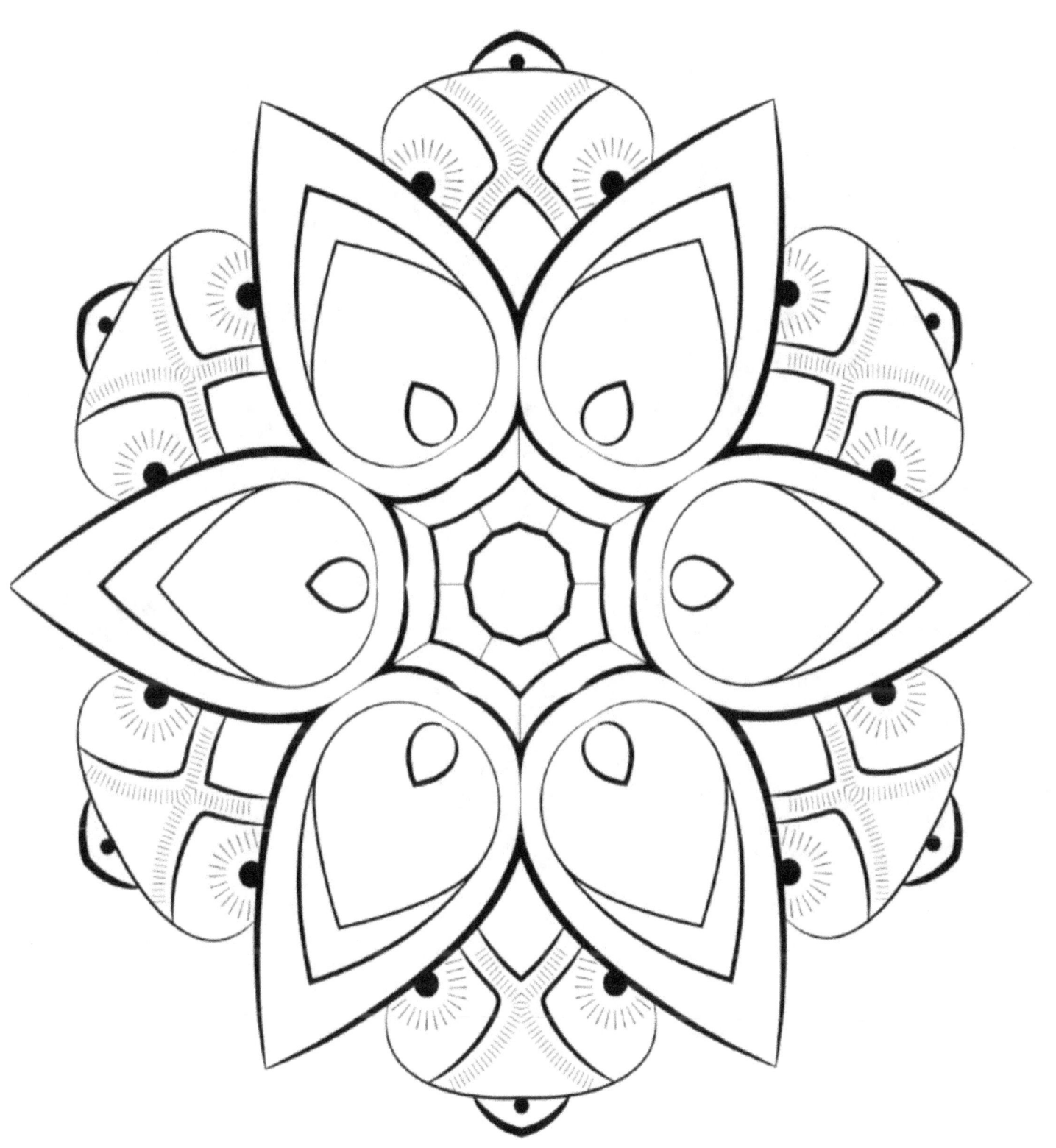

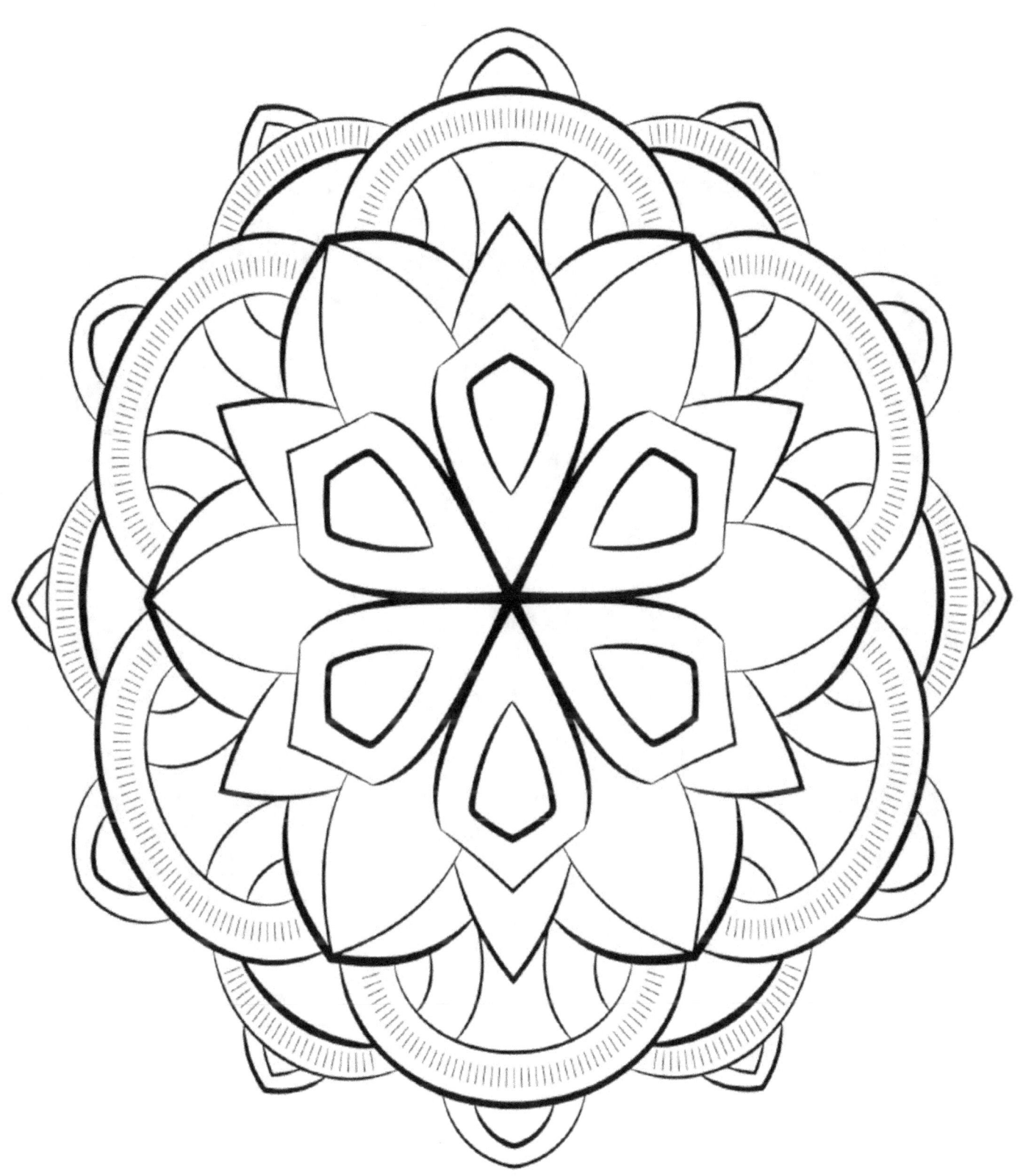

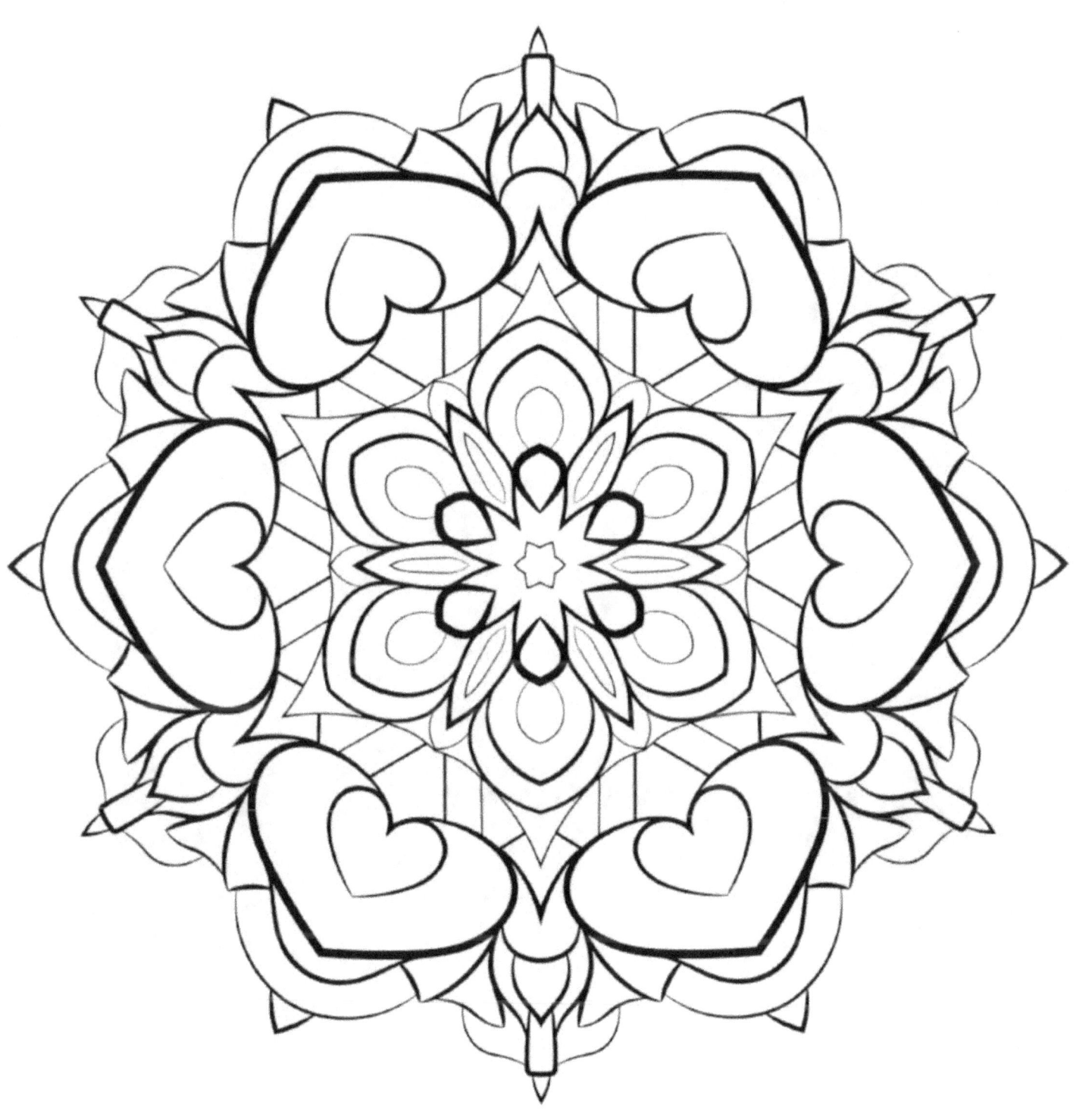

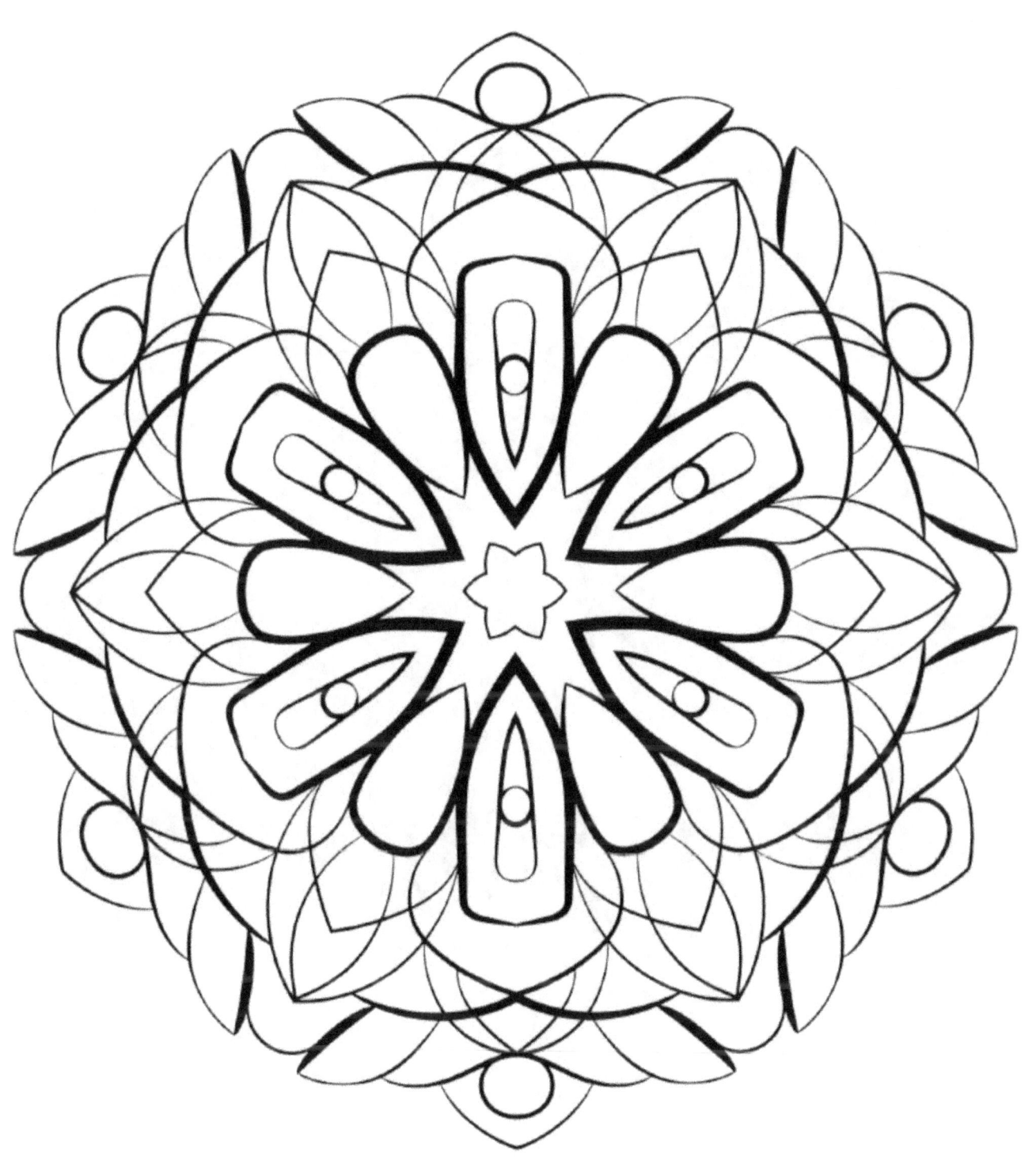

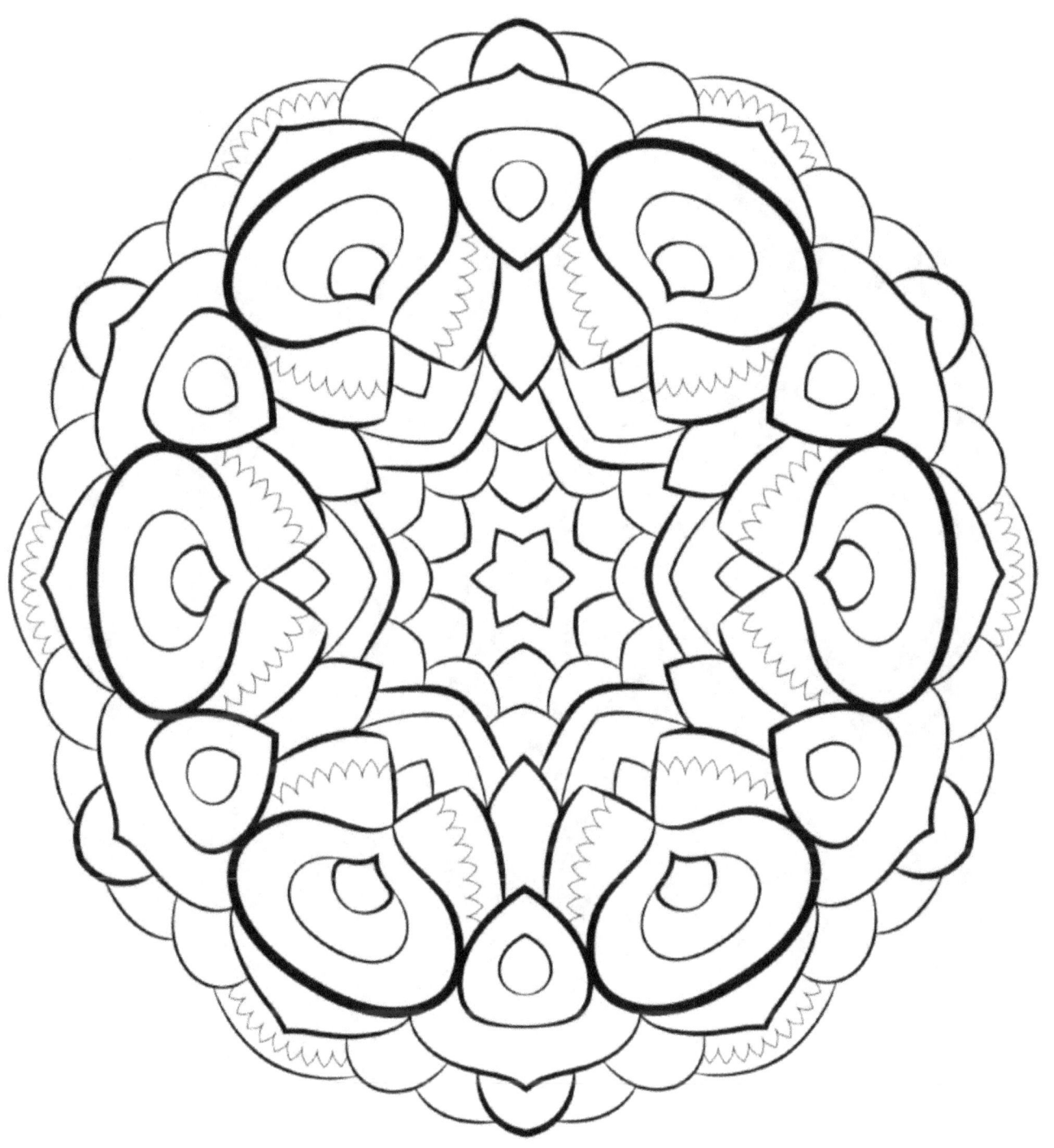

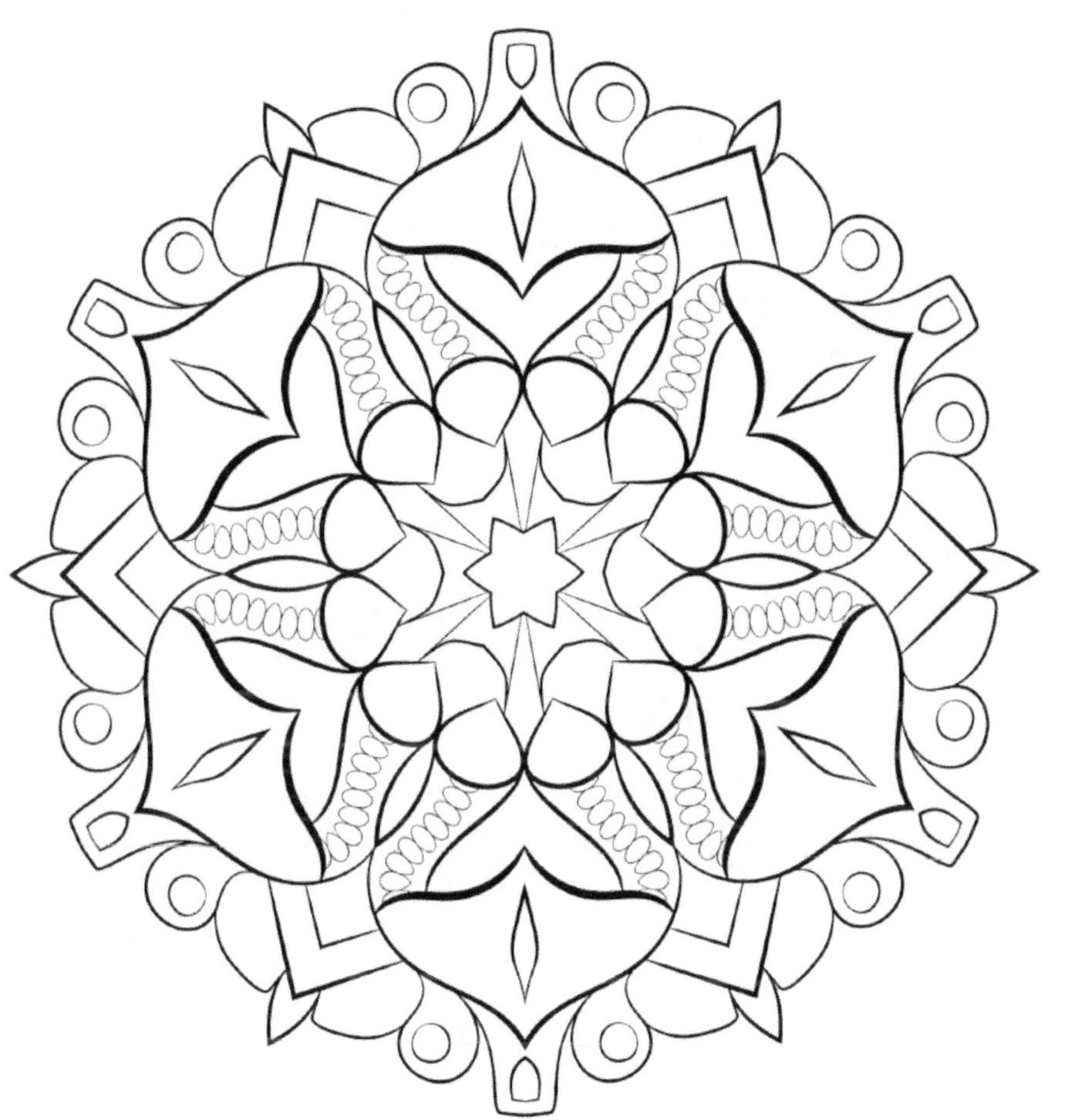

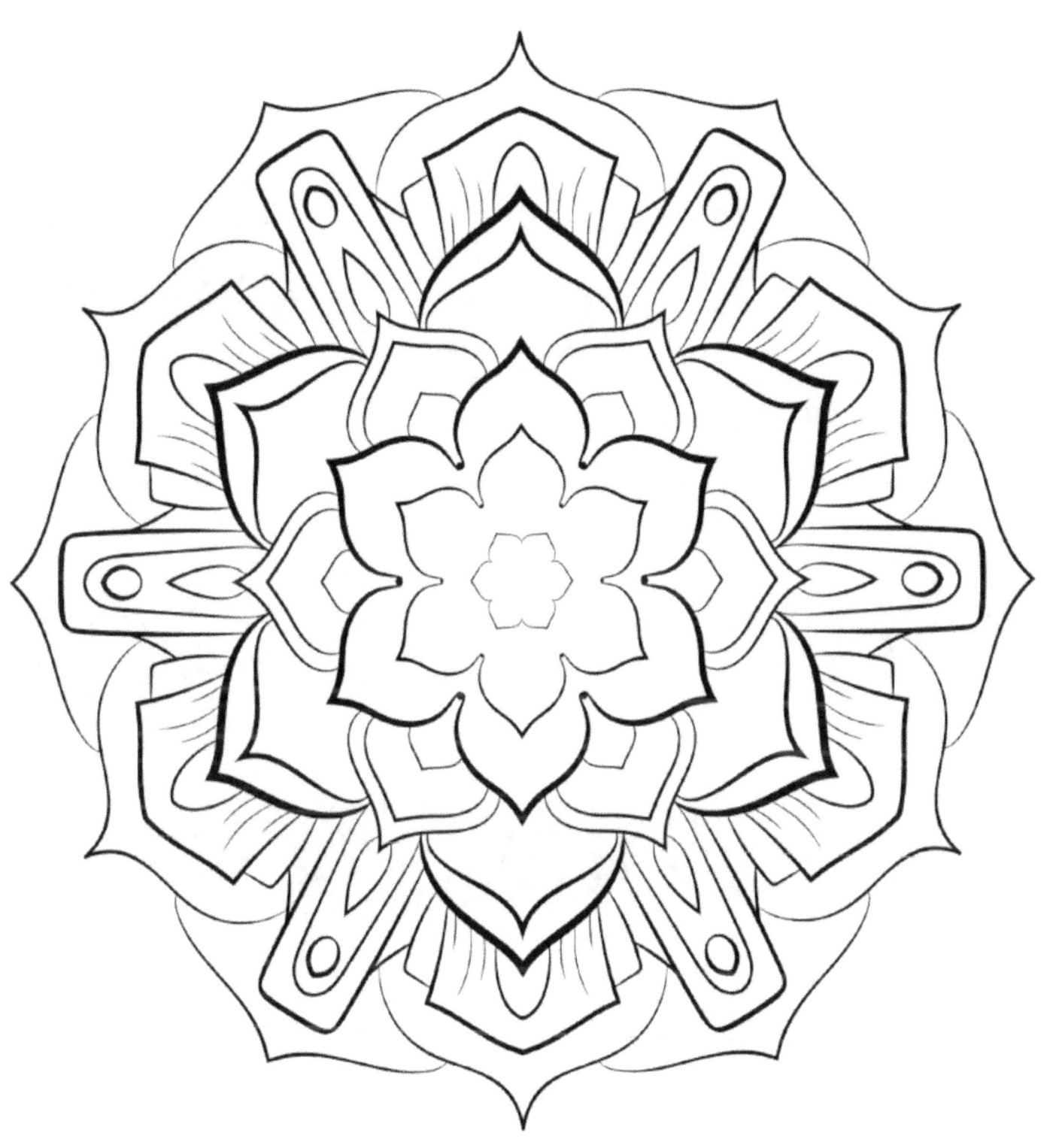

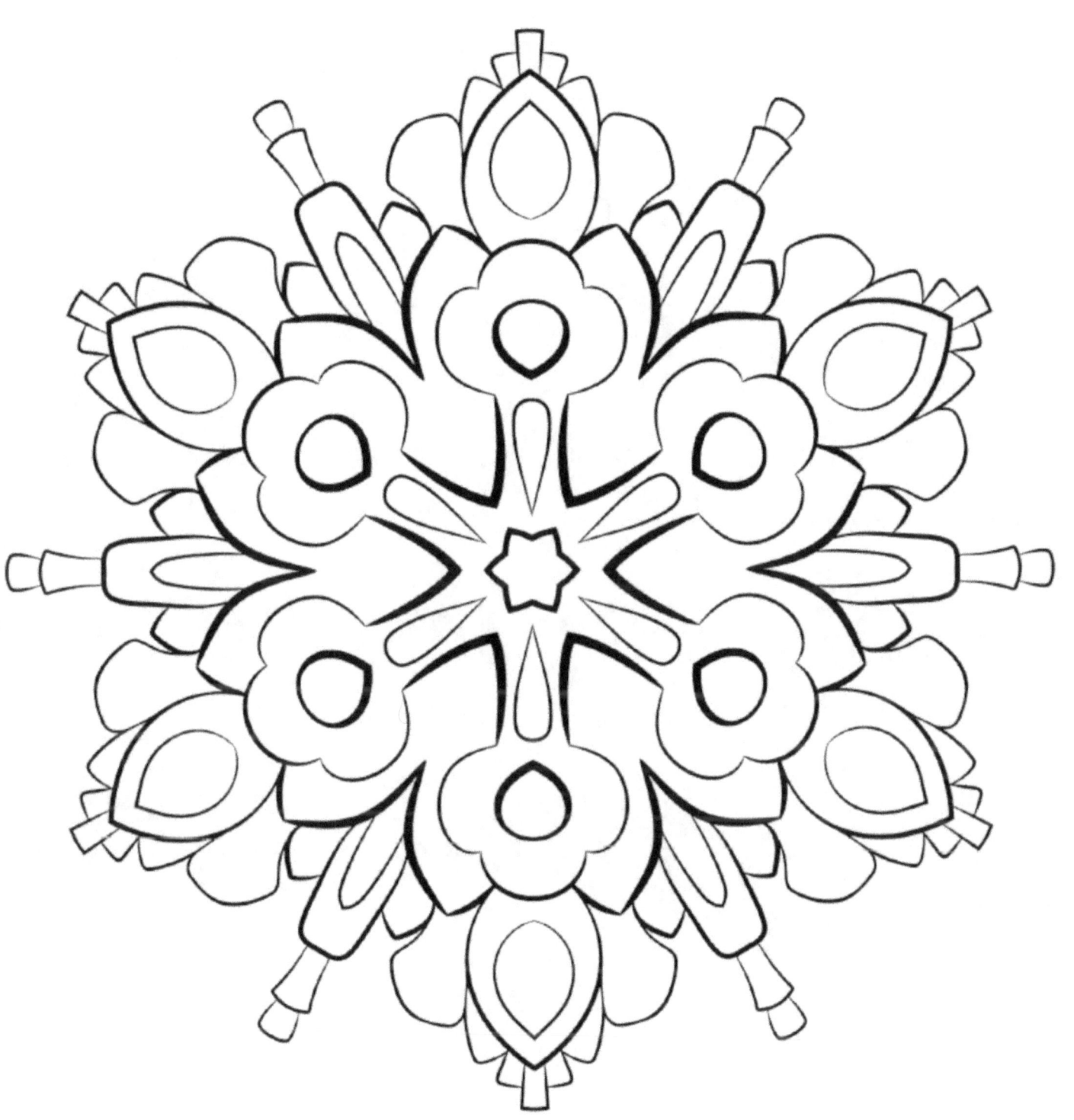

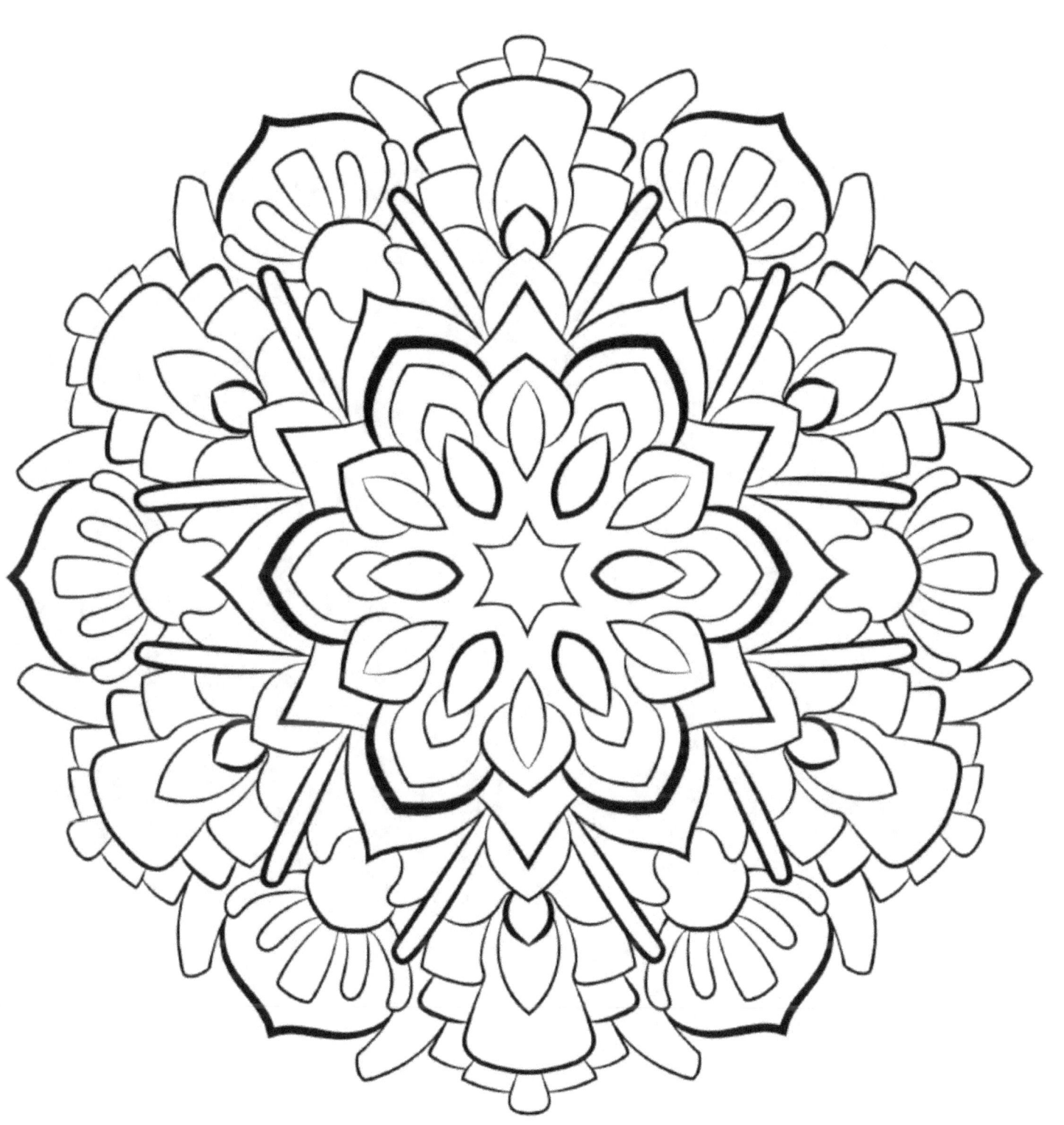

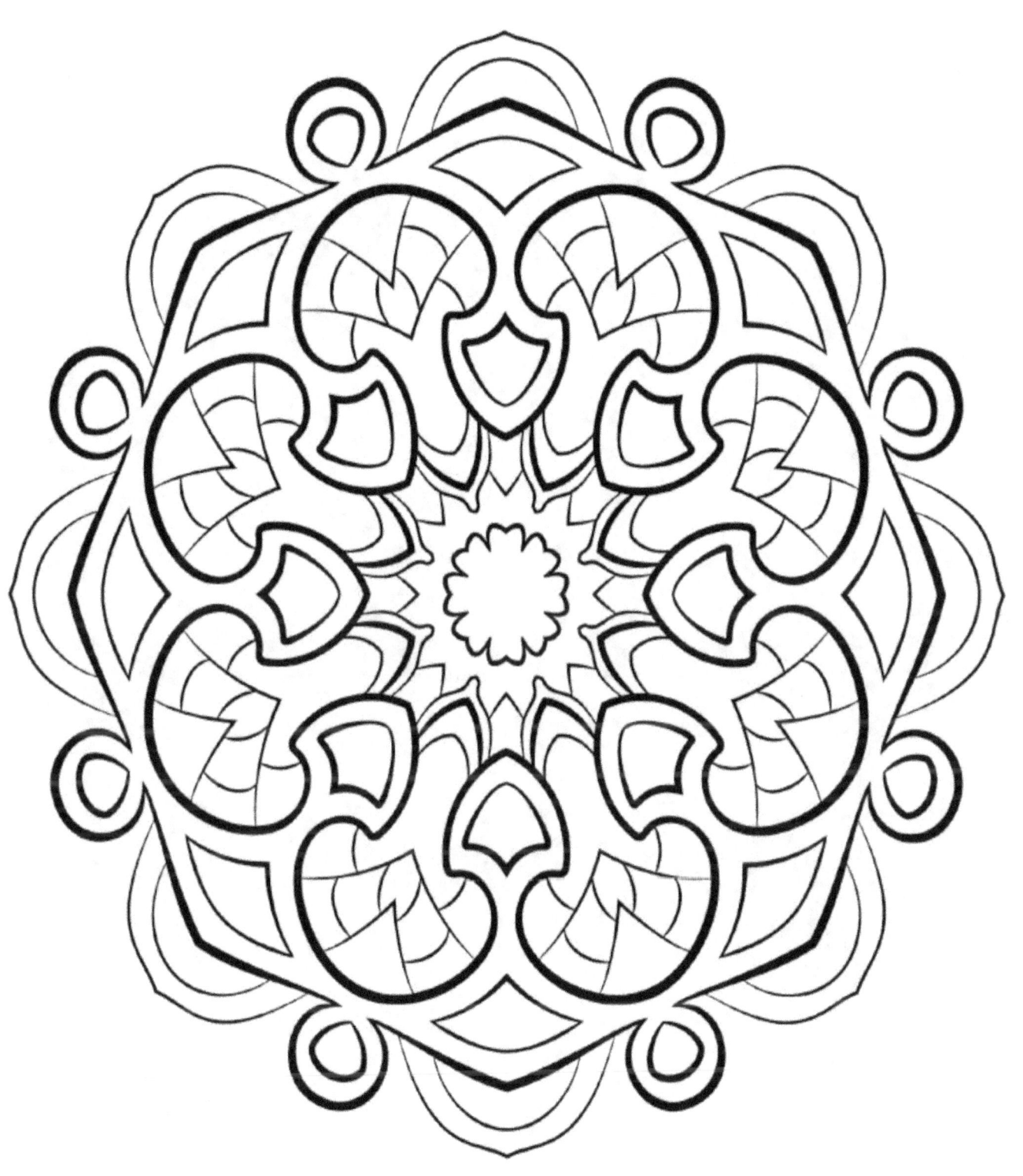

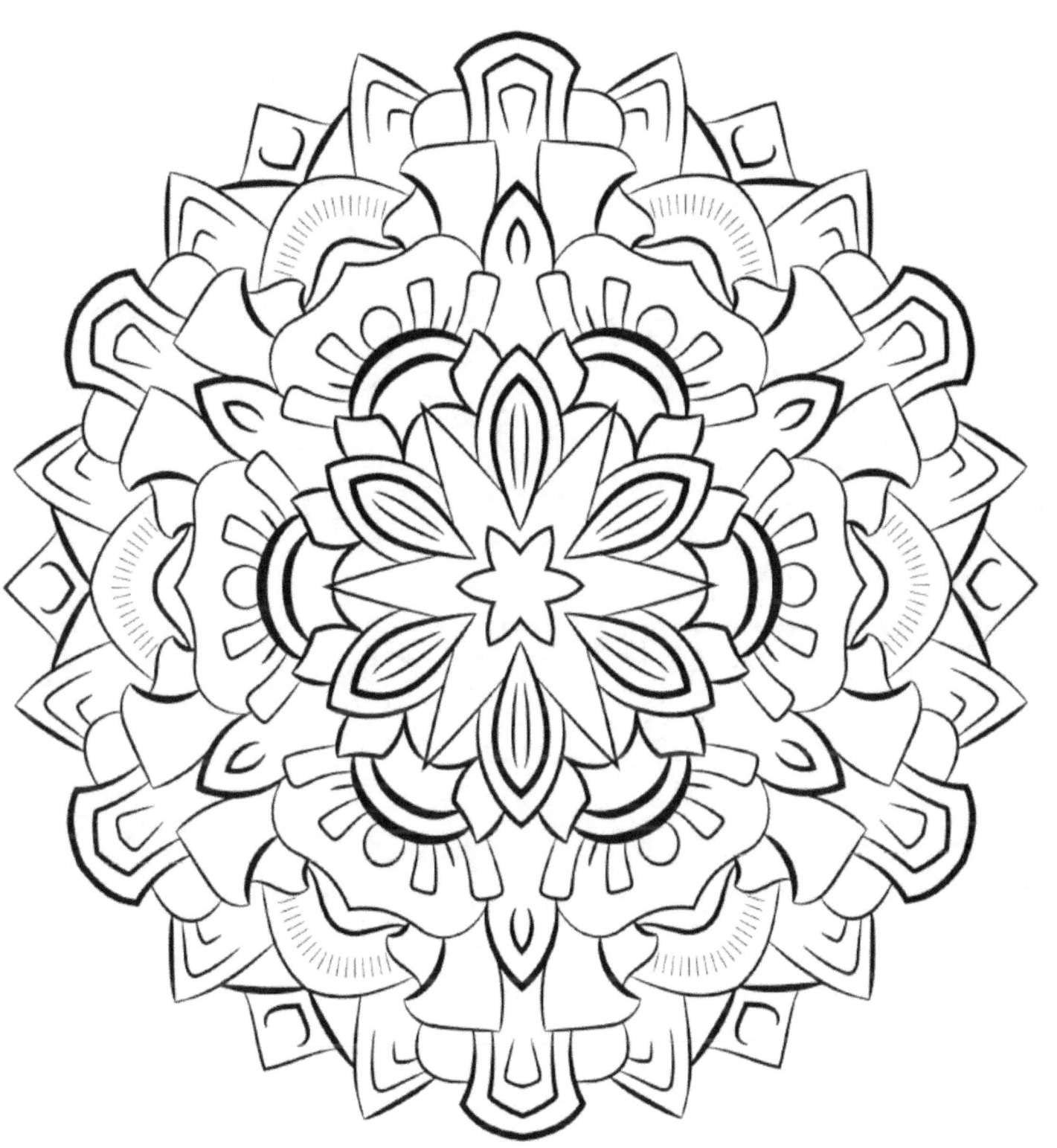

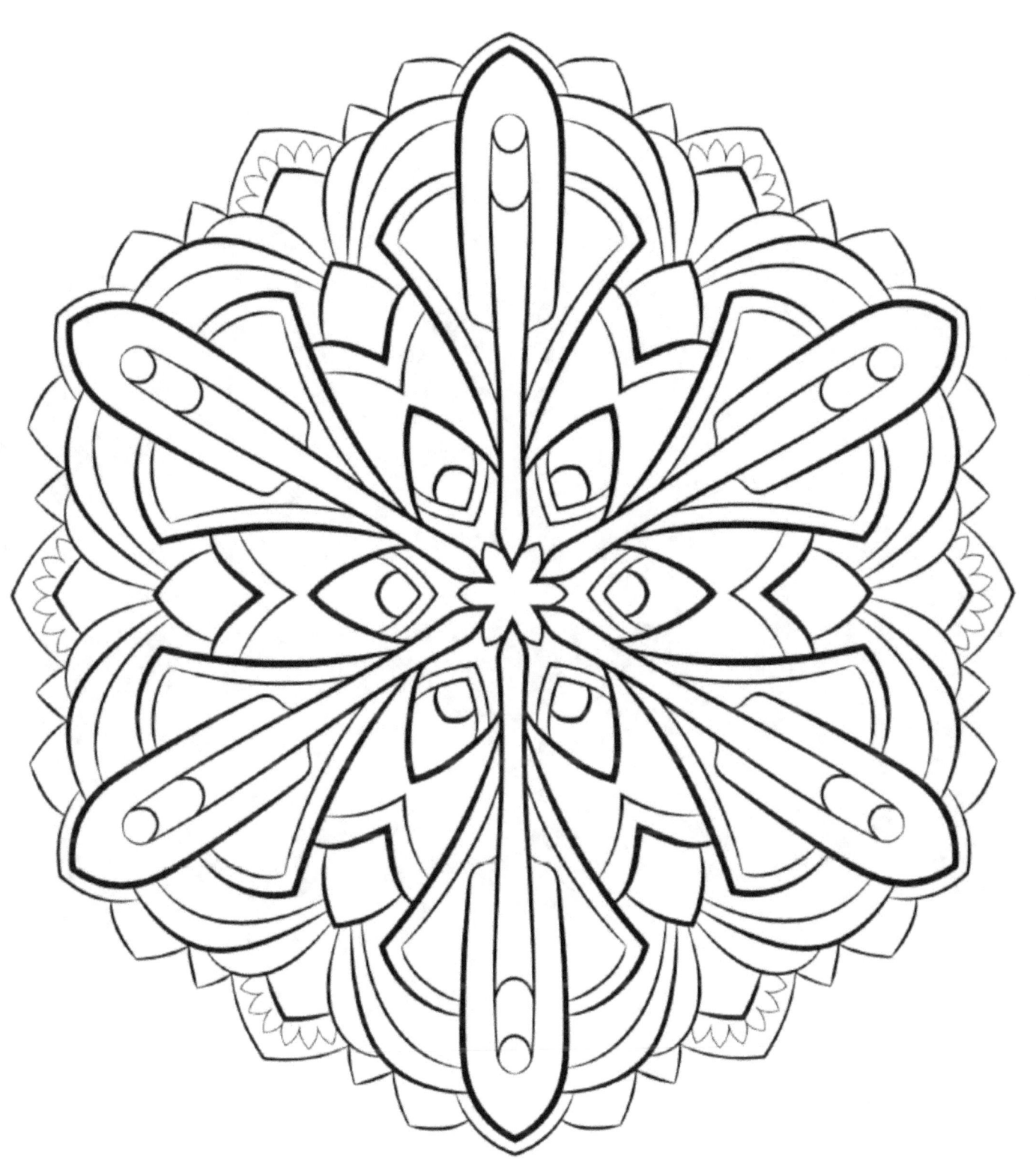

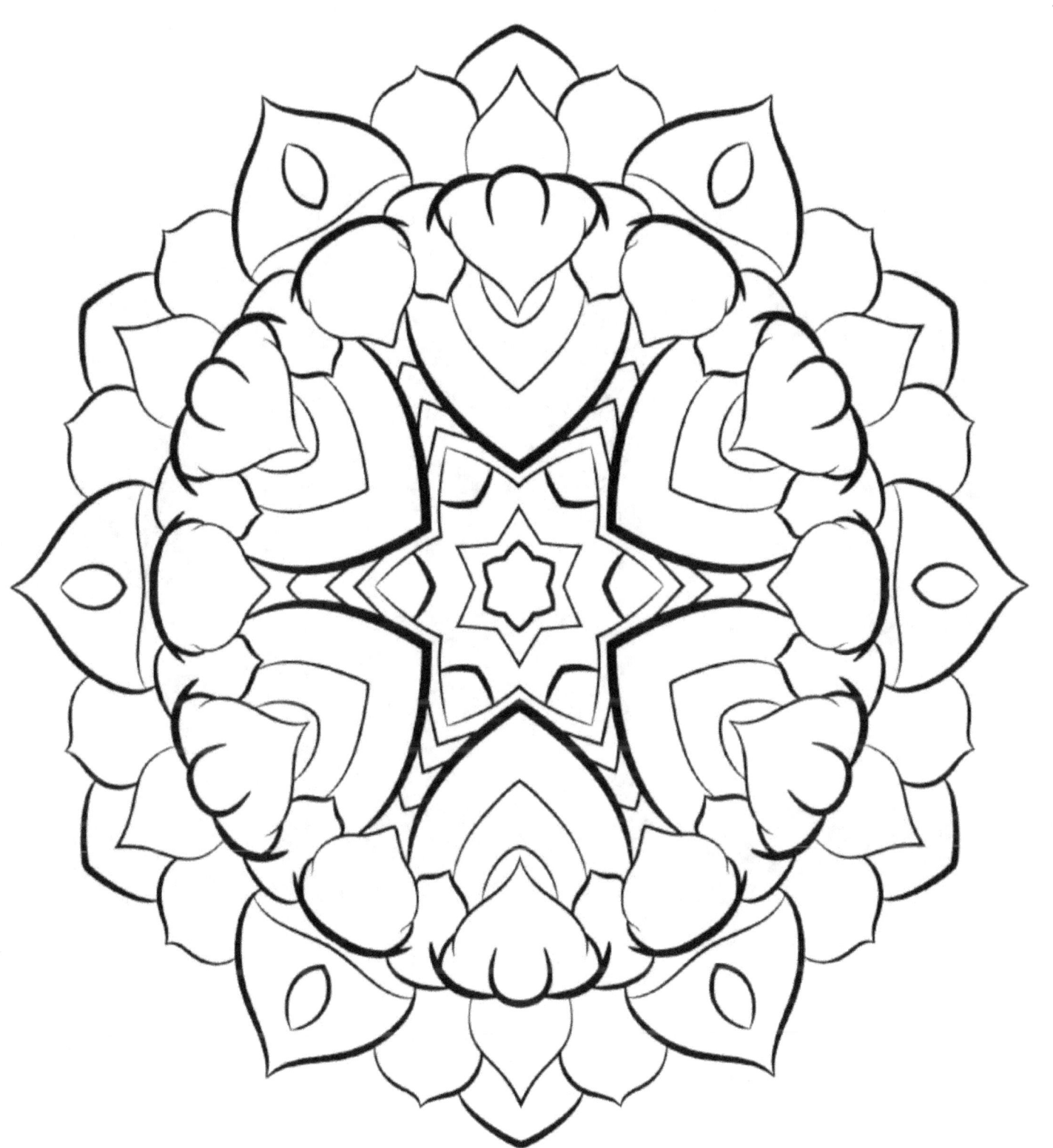

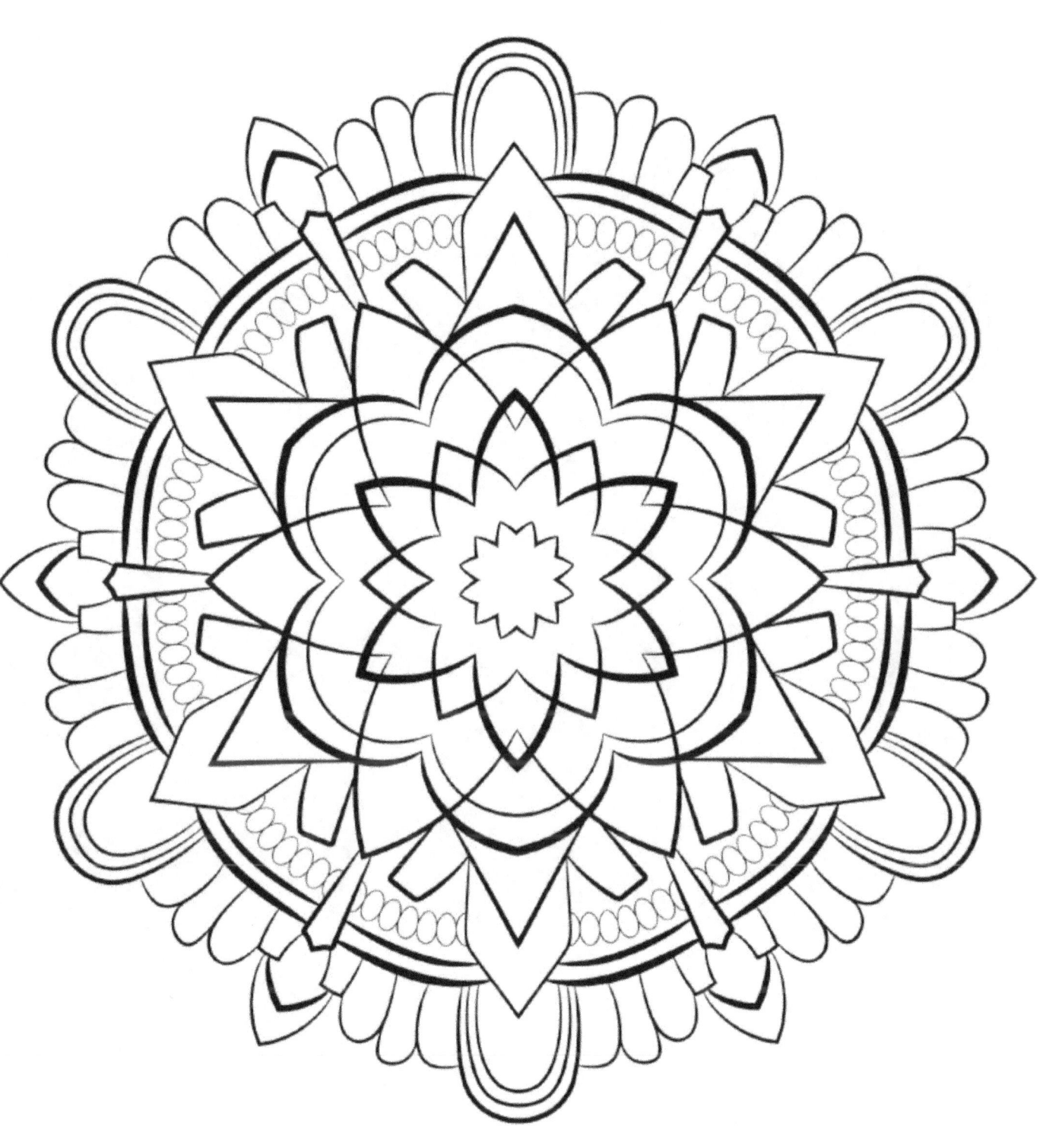

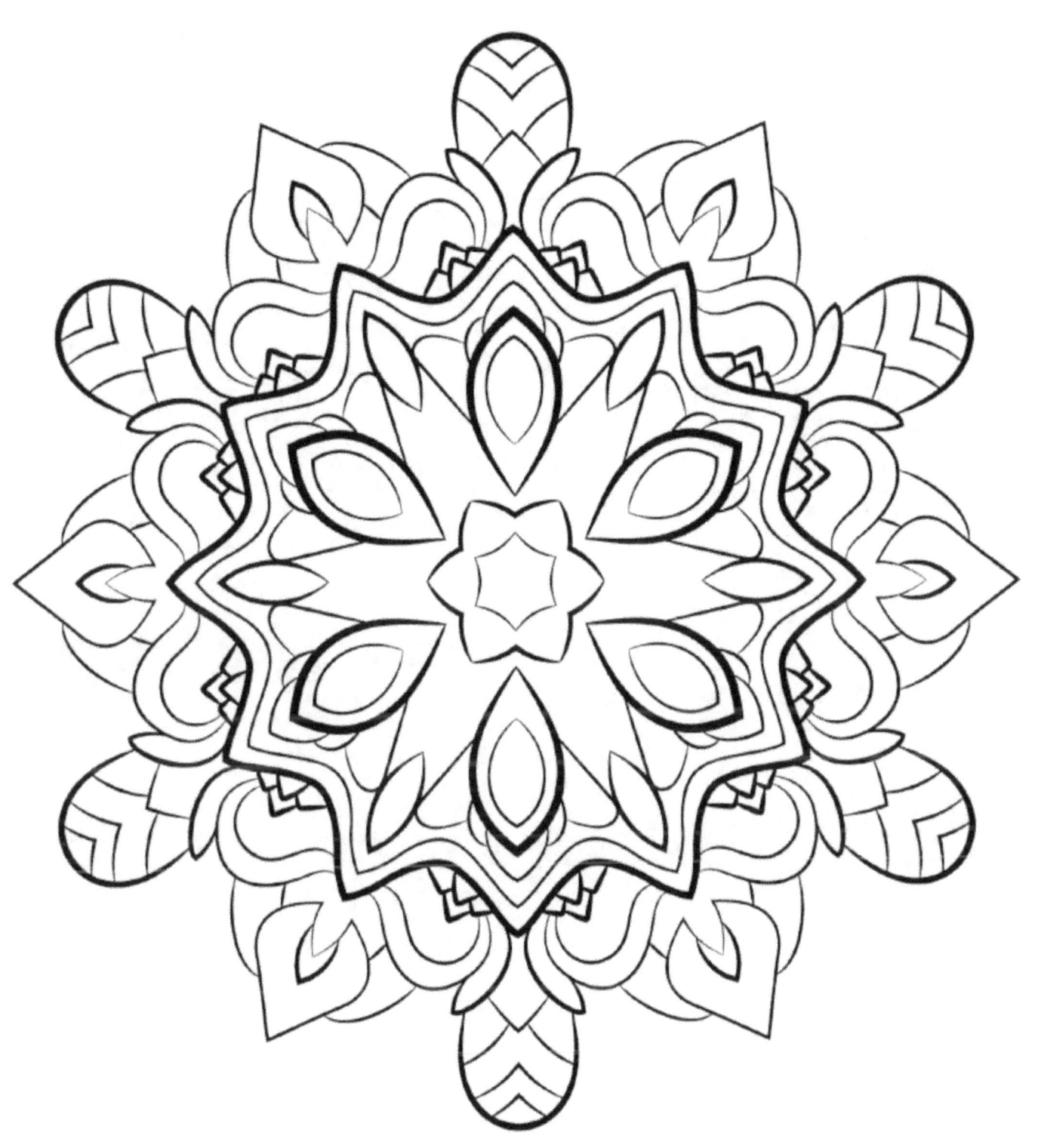

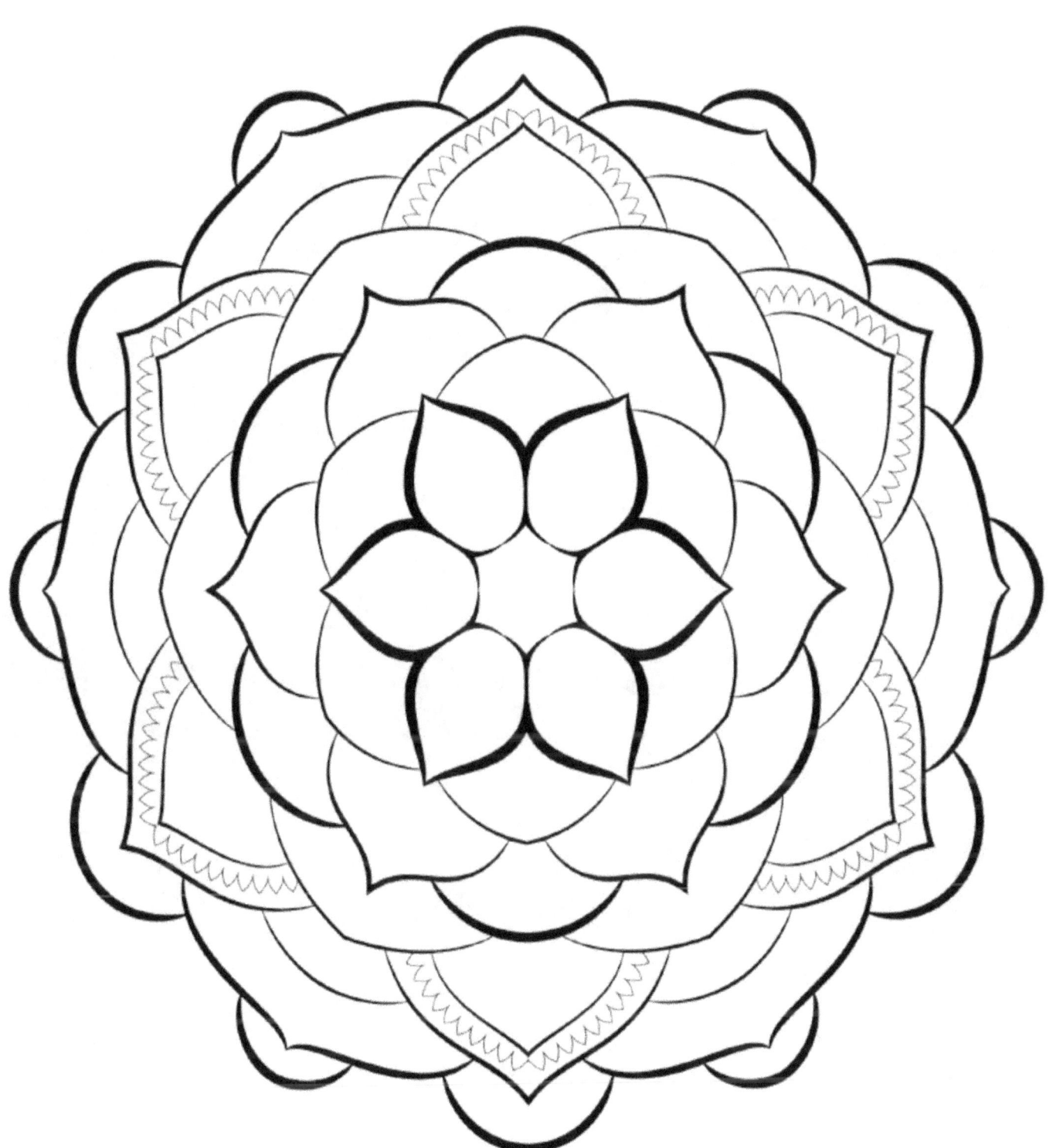

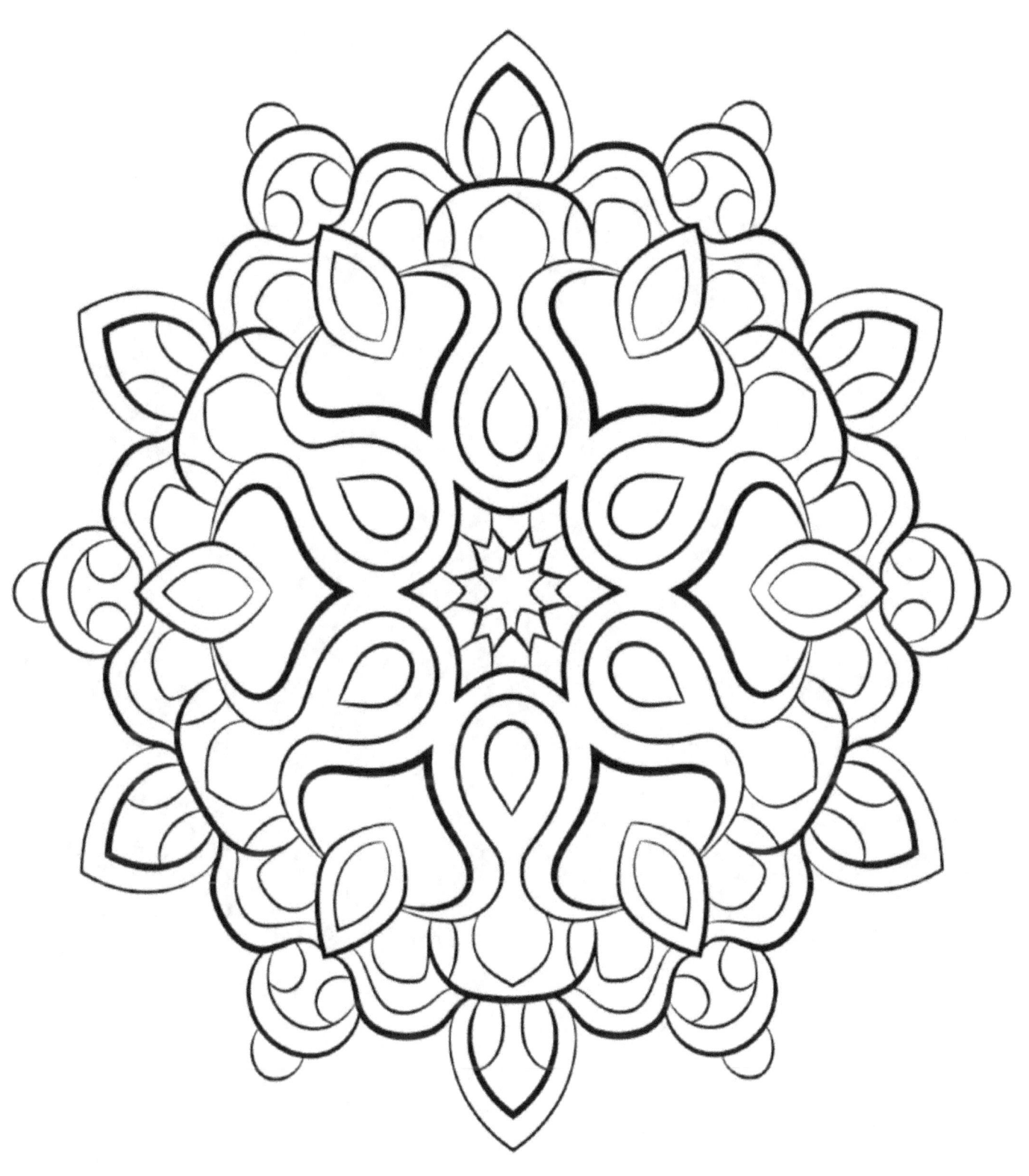

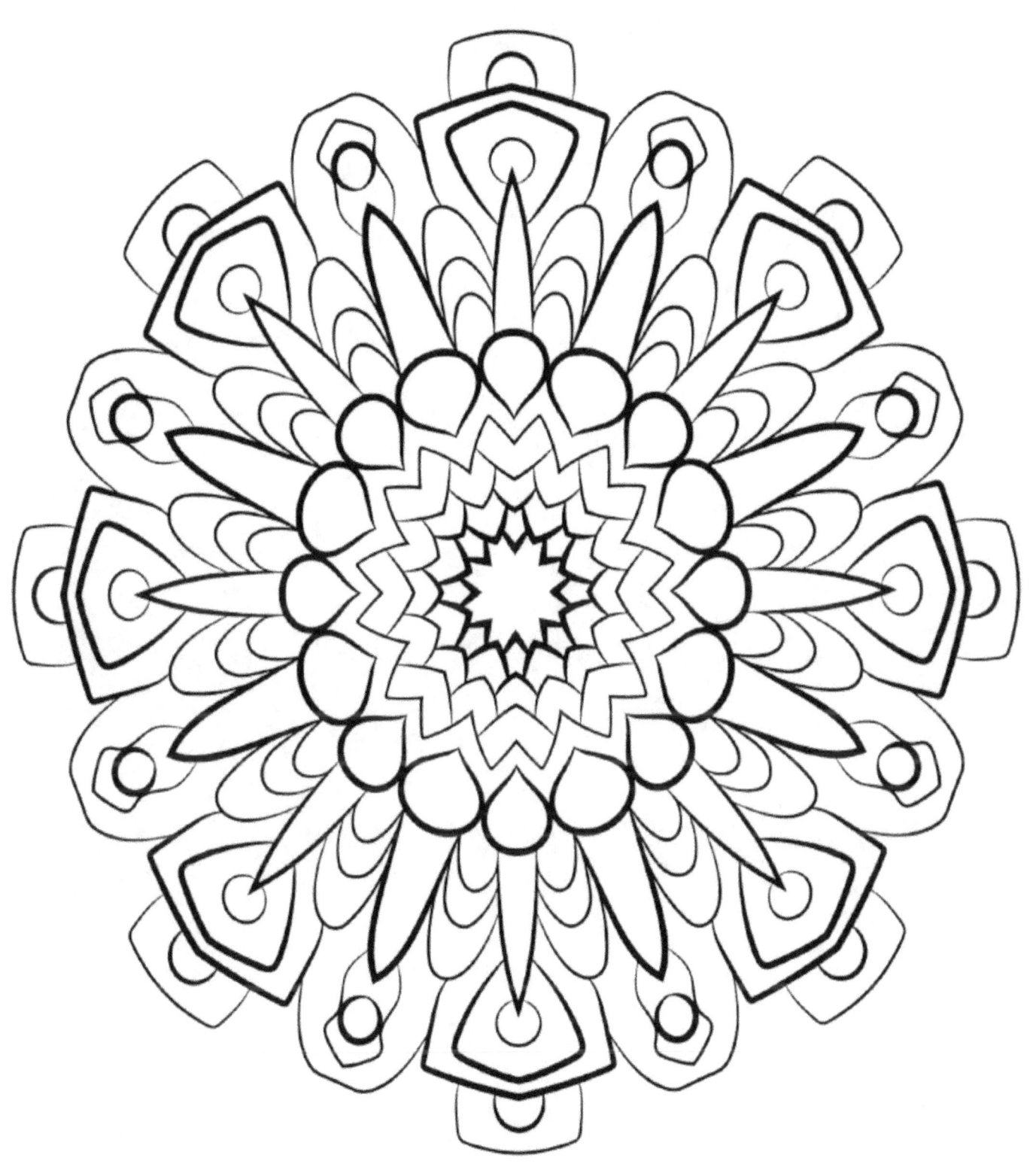

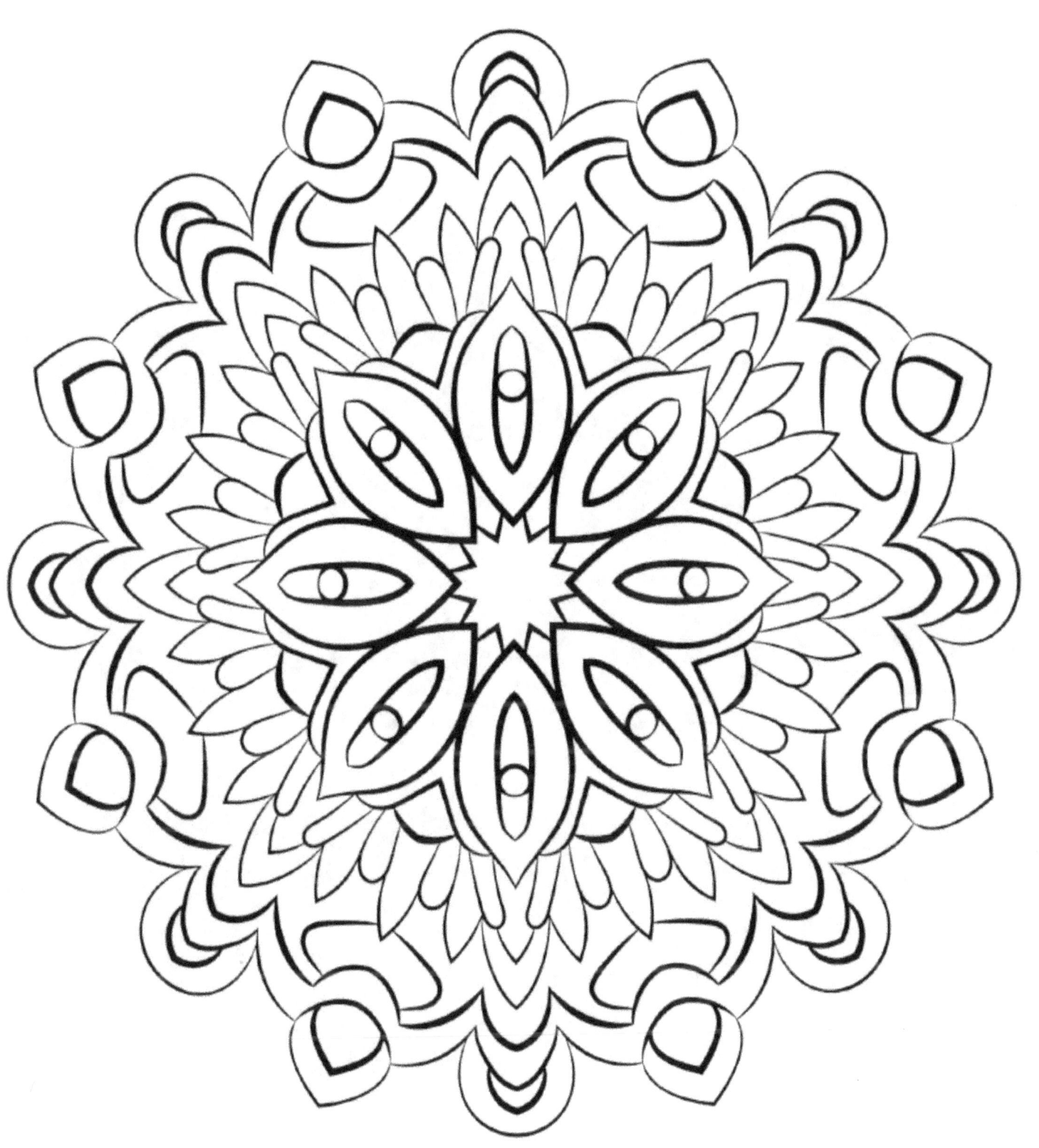

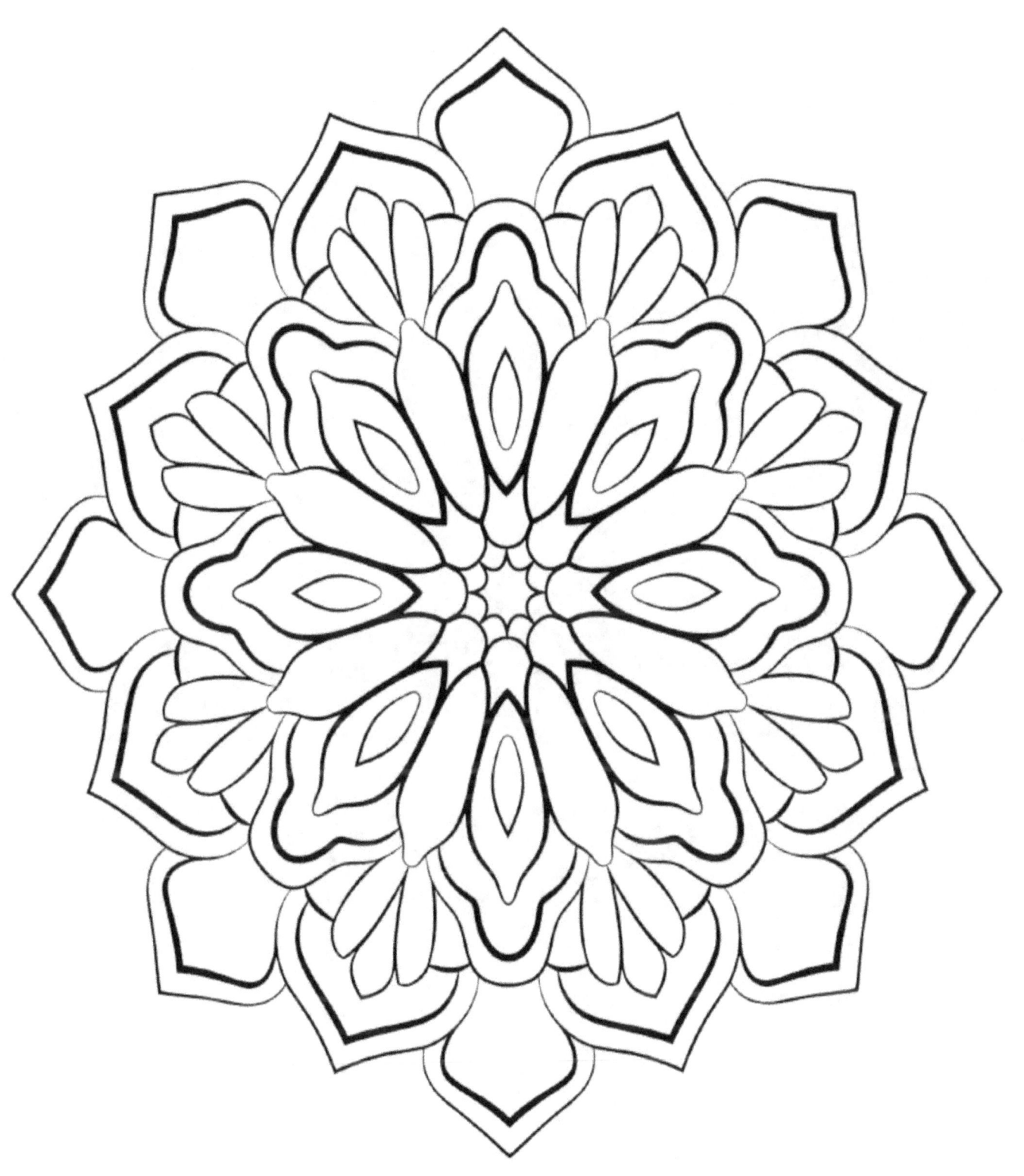

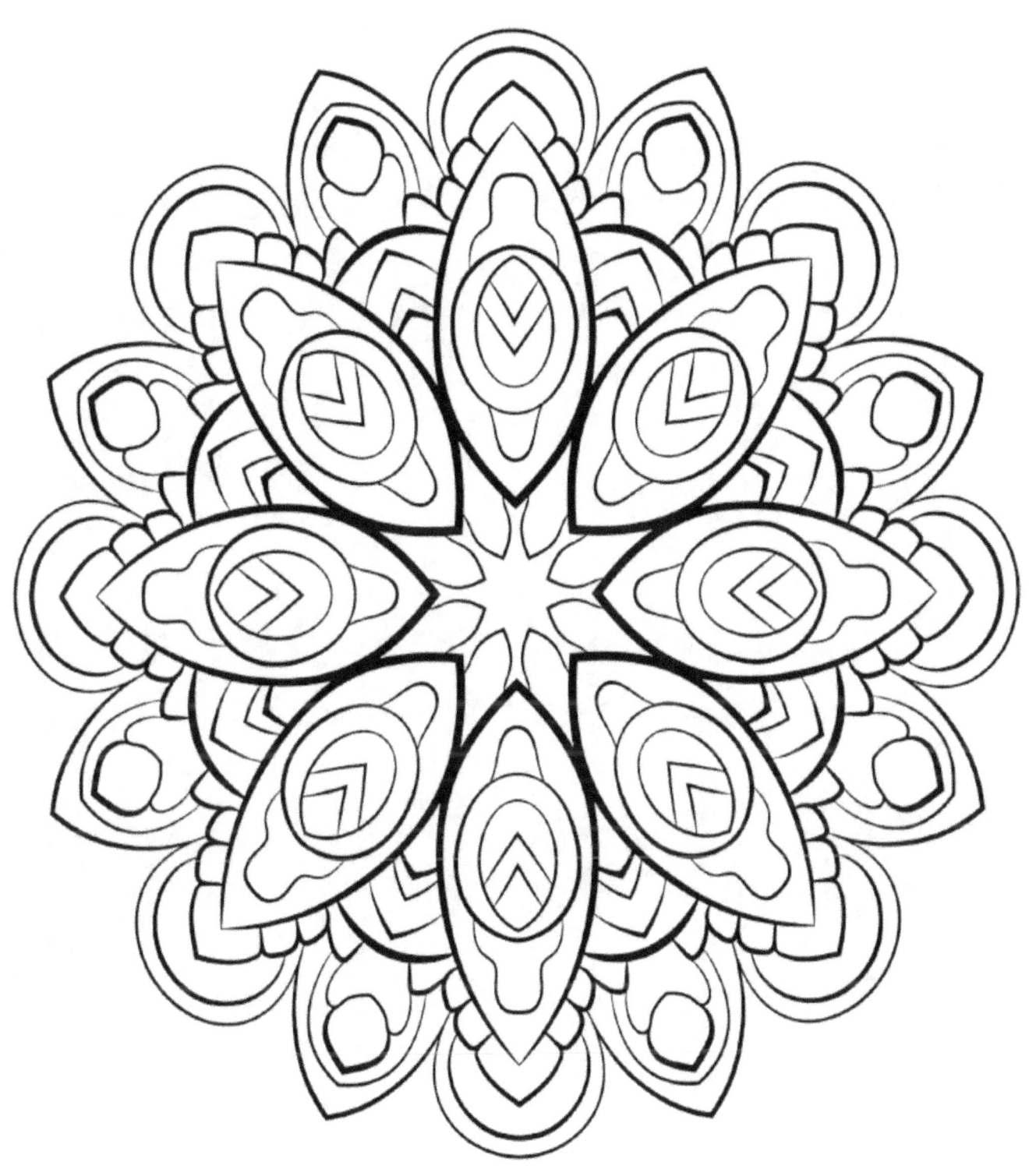

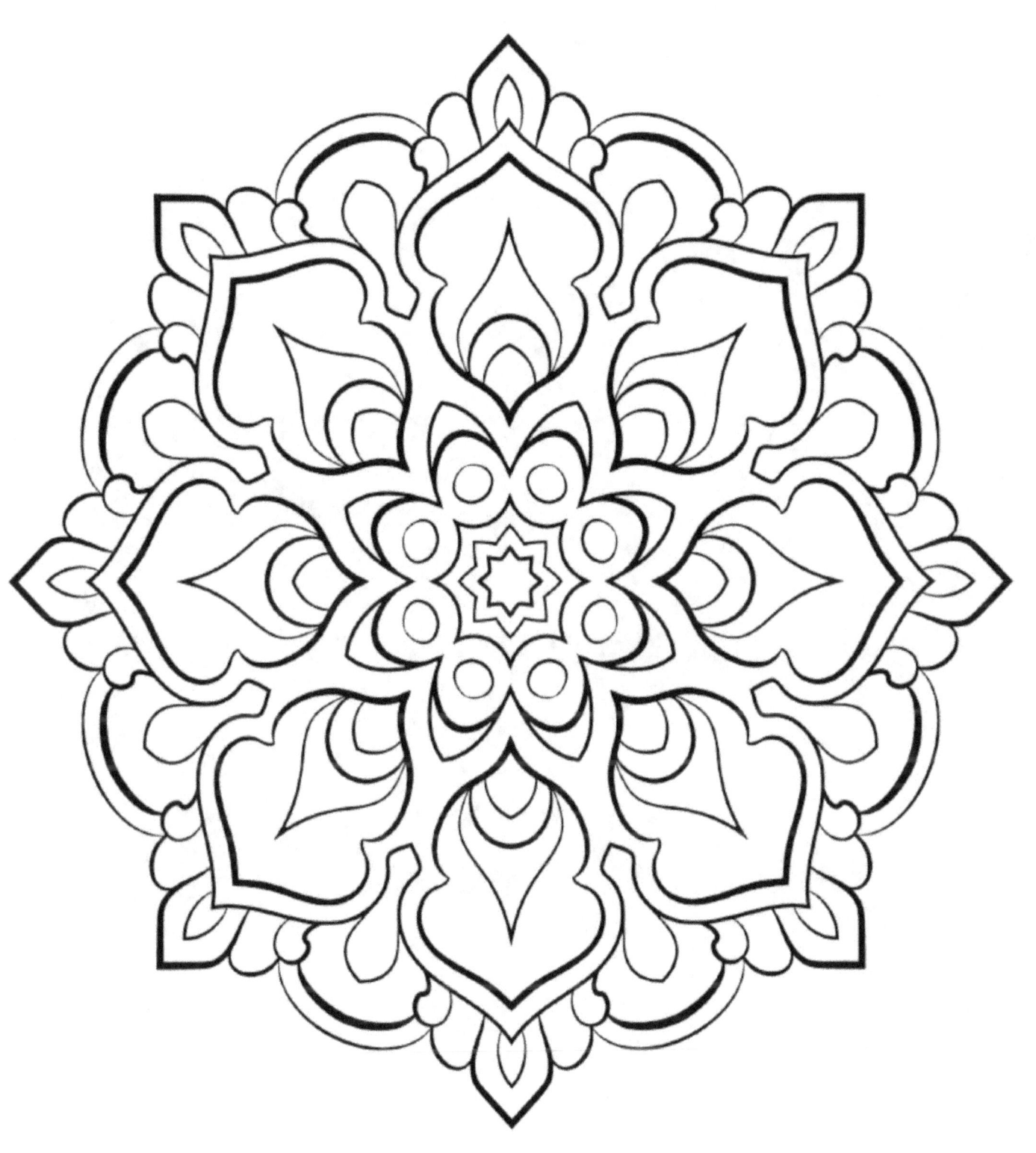

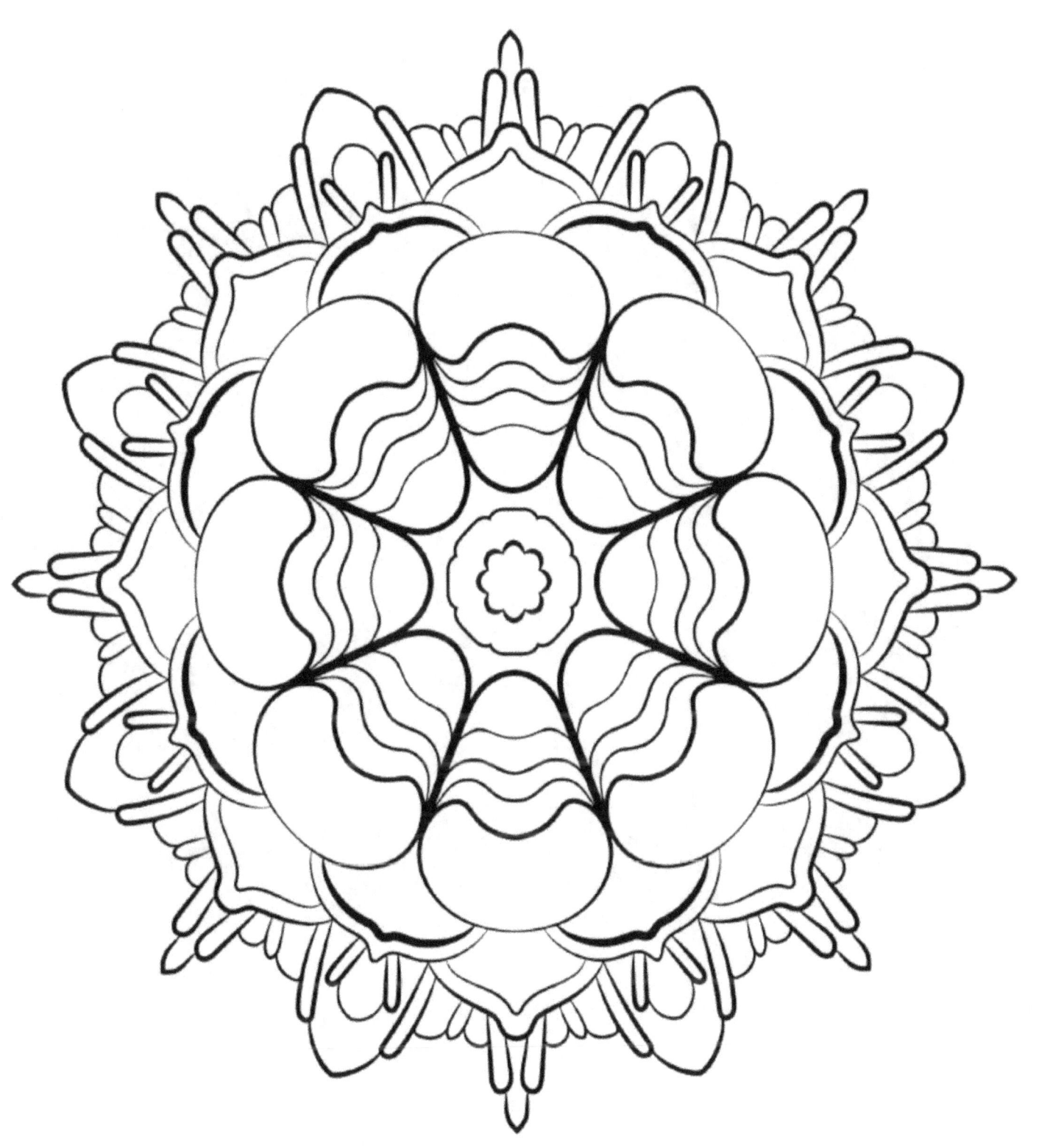

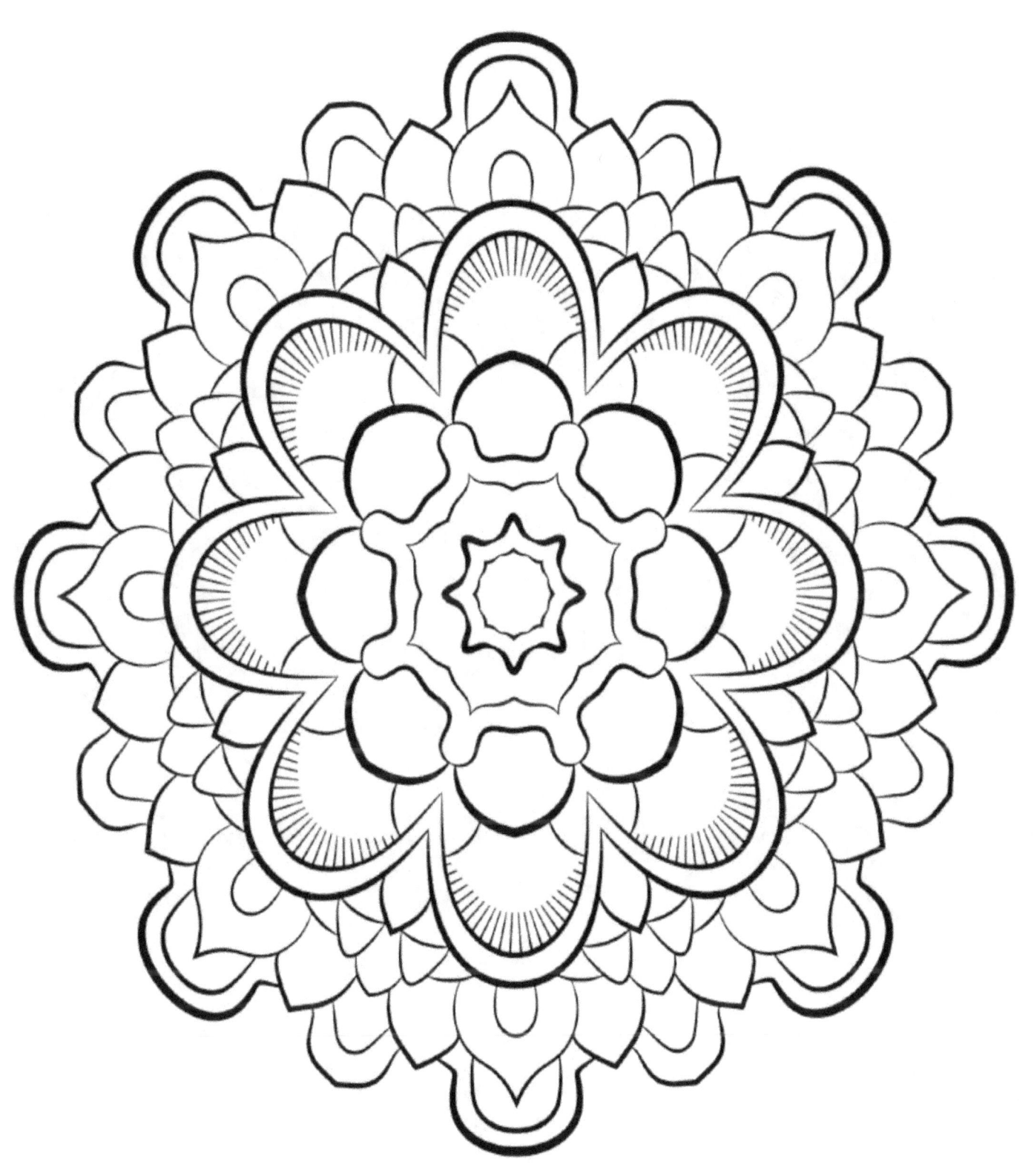

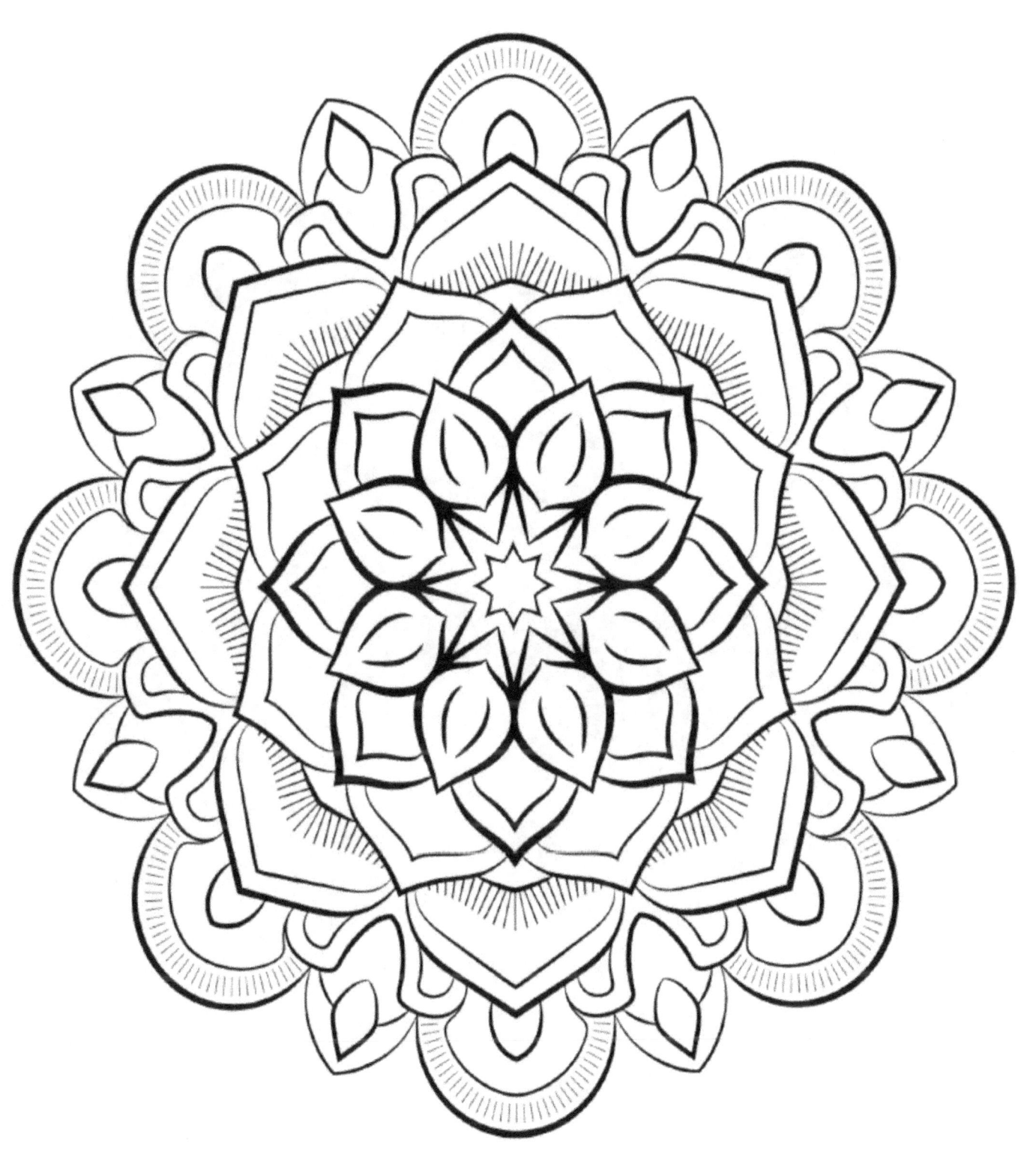

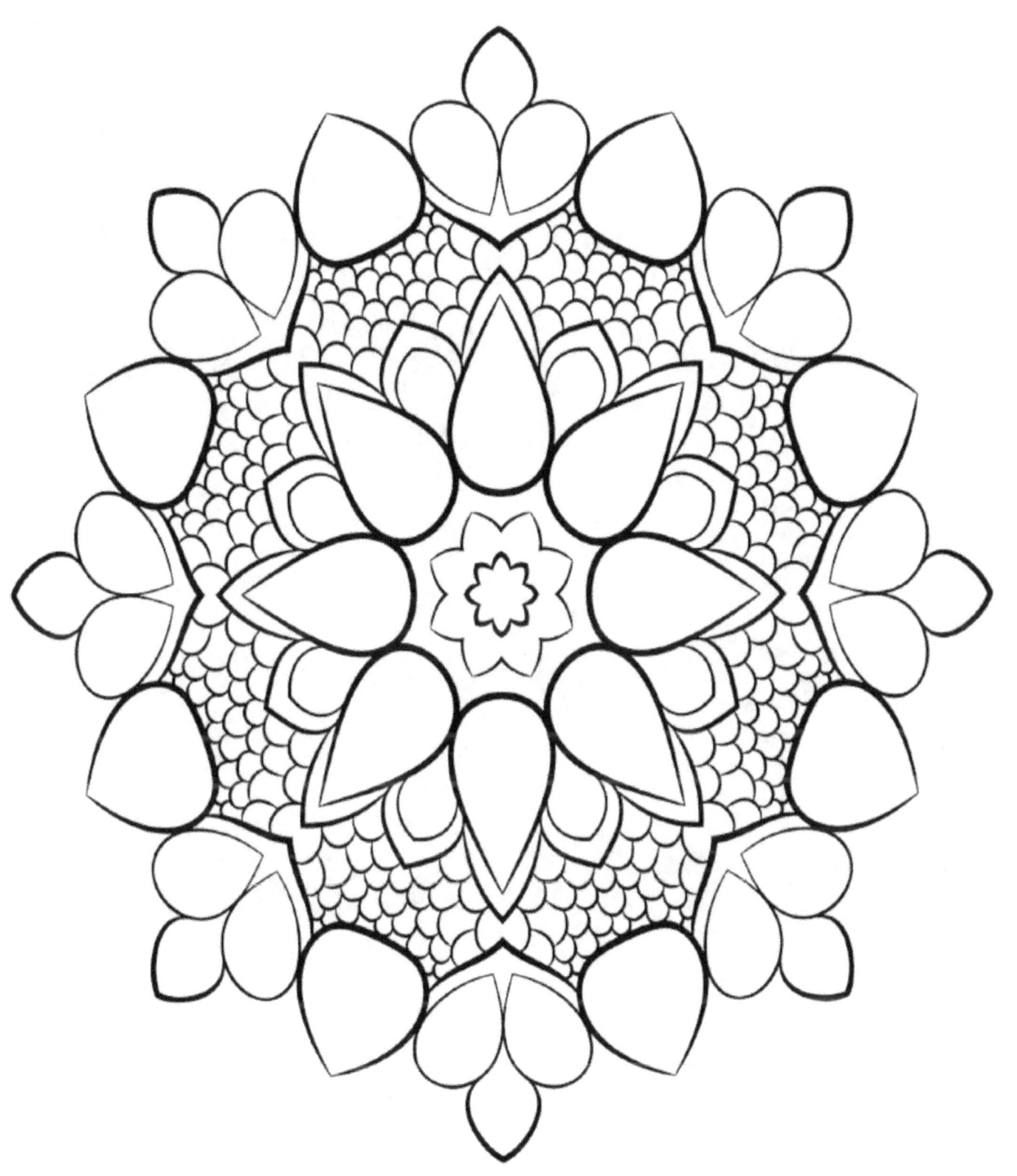

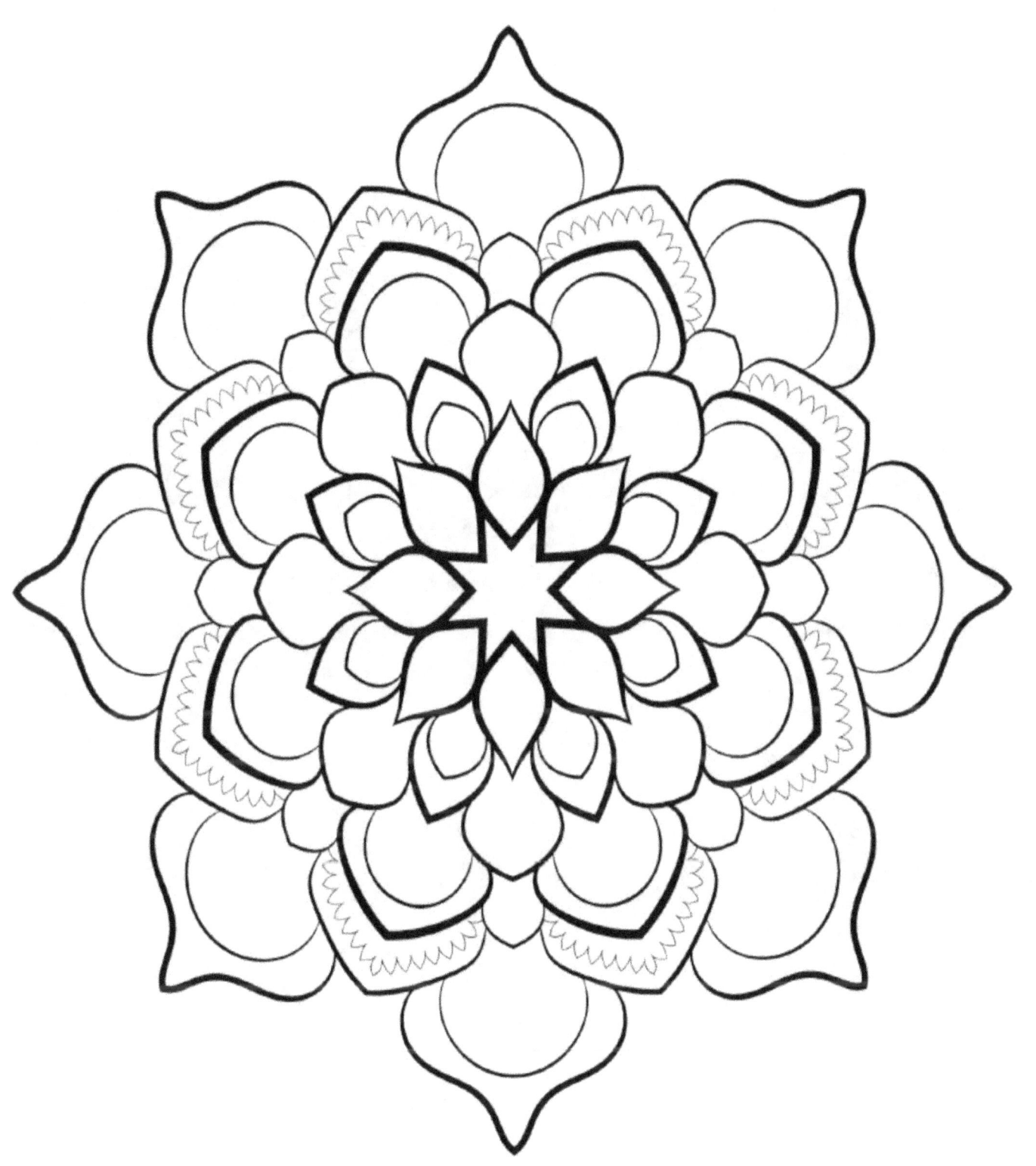

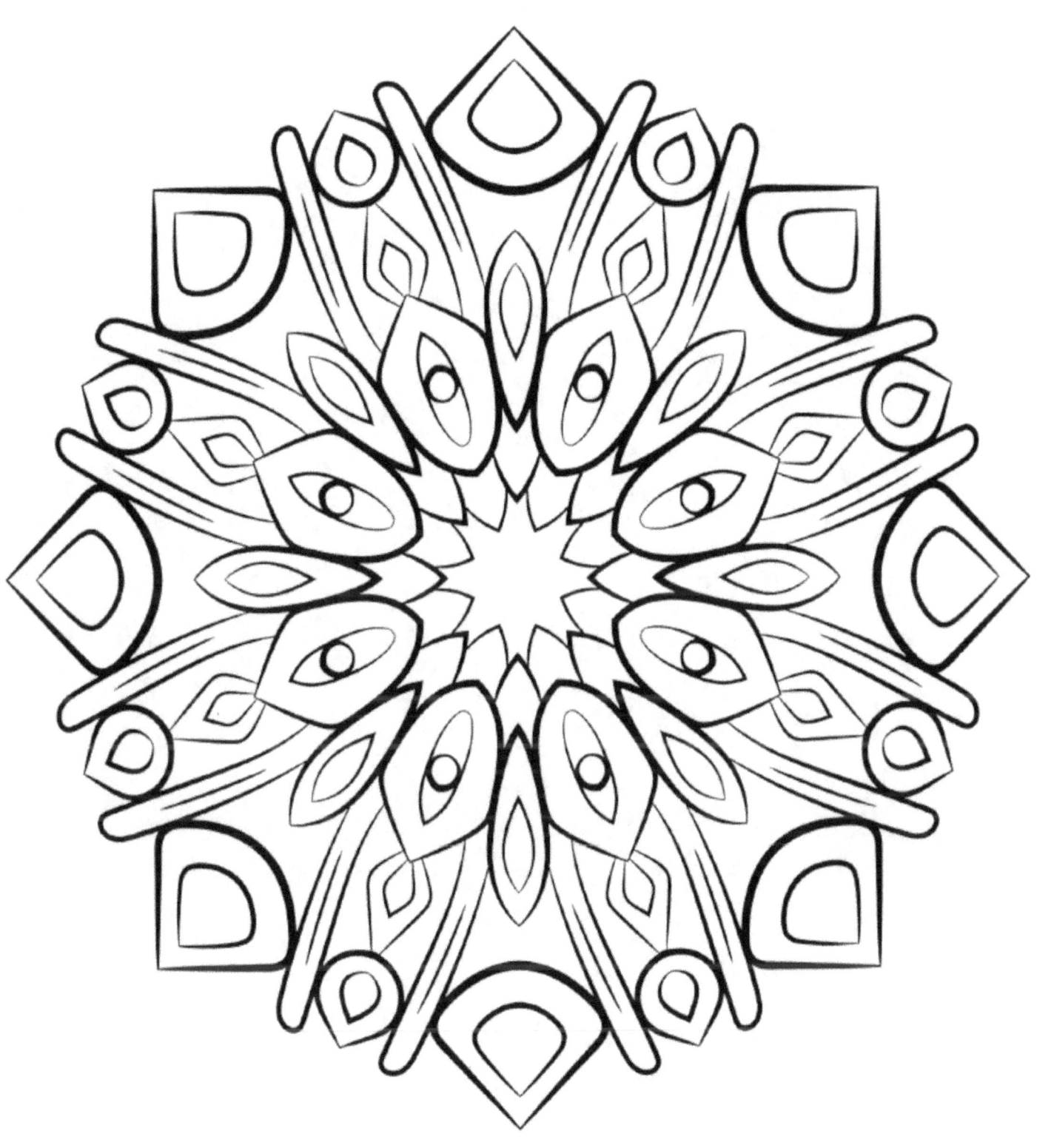

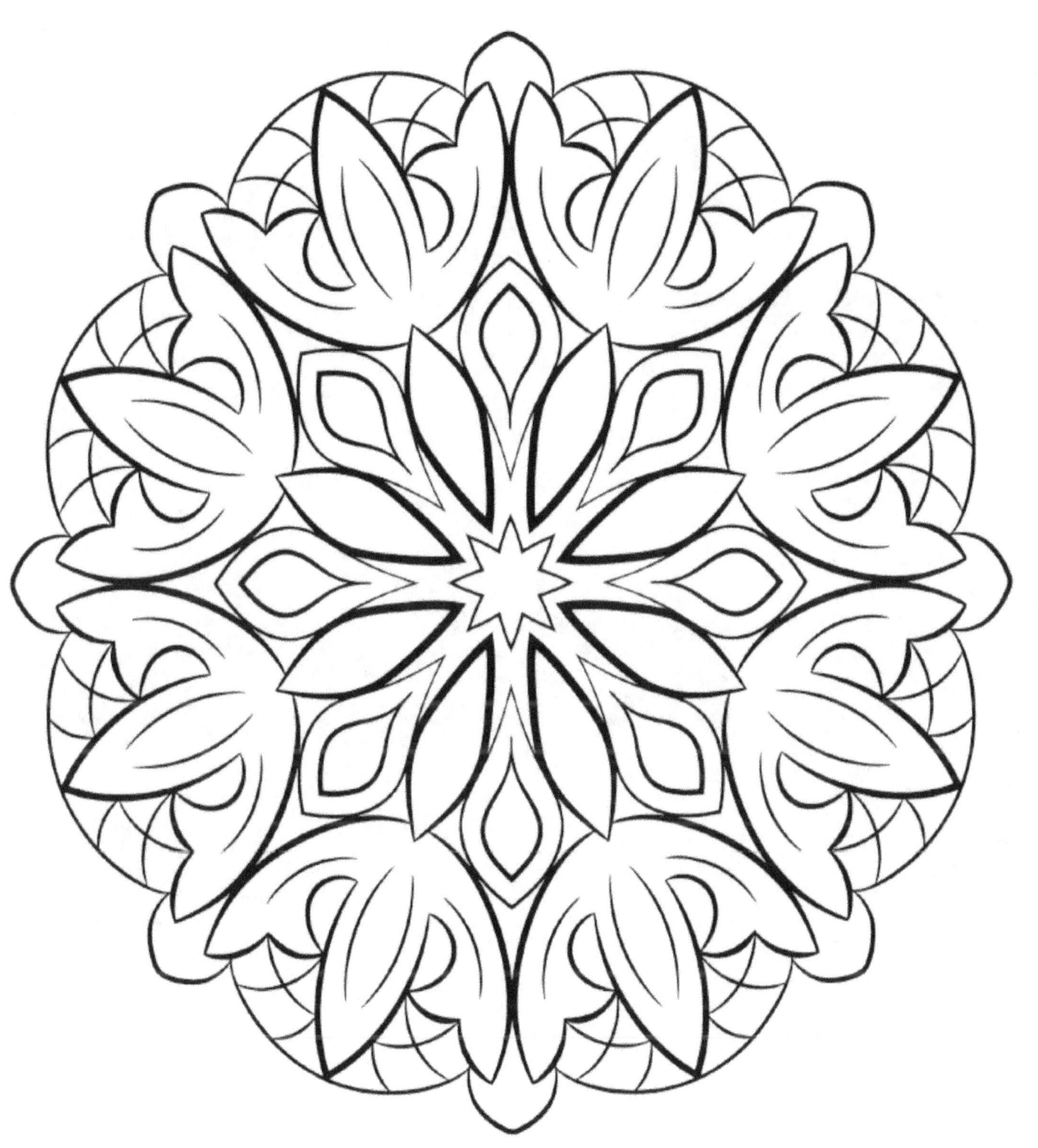

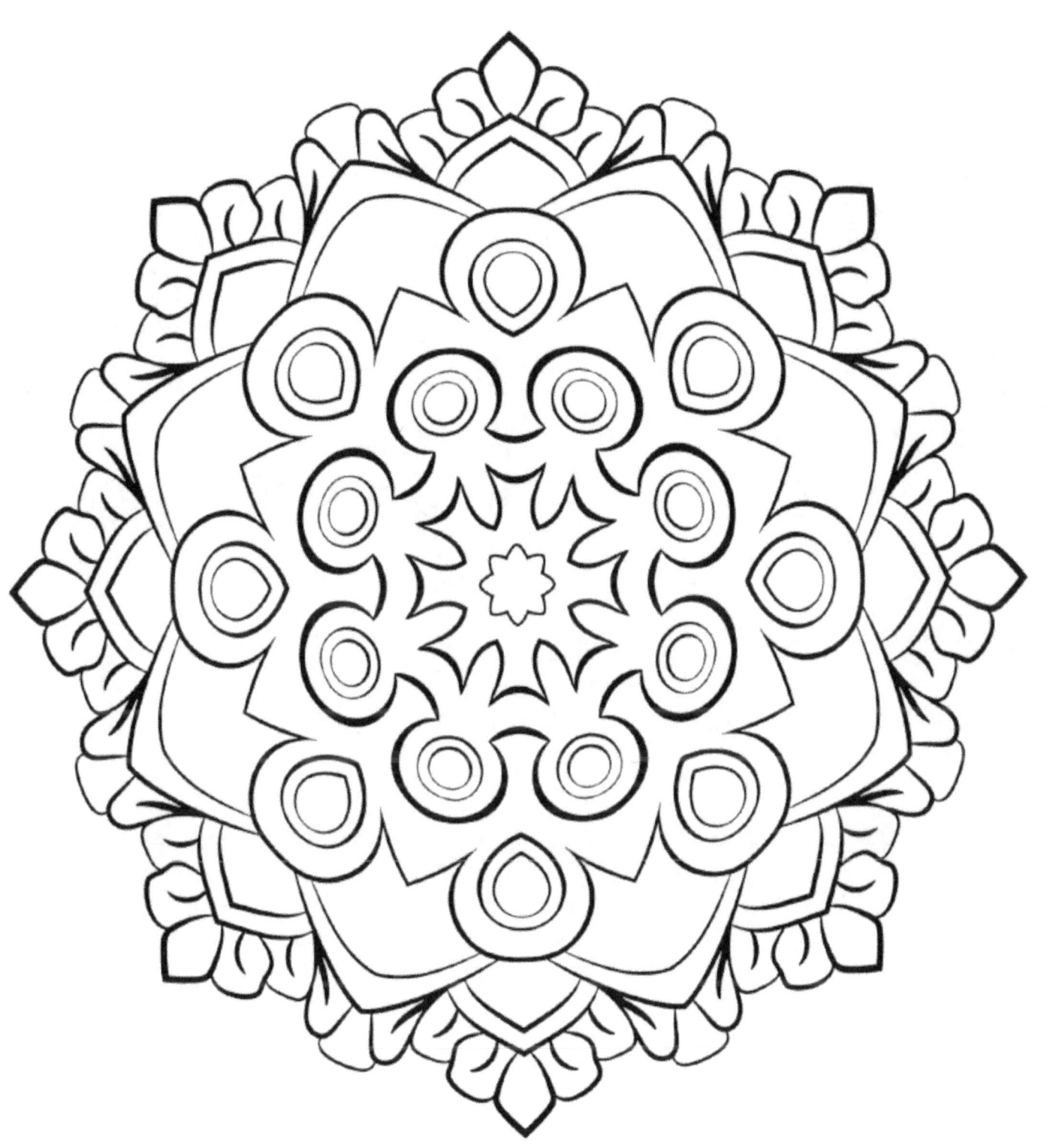

www.ingramcontent.com/pod-product-compliance
Lightning Source LLC
Chambersburg PA
CBHW080834170526
45158CB00009B/2563